MW01054445

A HISTORICAL JOURNEY
ACROSS
RARITAN BAY

A HISTORICAL JOURNEY
═ ACROSS ═
RARITAN BAY

JOHN SCHNEIDER

THE
History
PRESS

Published by The History Press
Charleston, SC
www.historypress.com

Copyright © 2020 by John Schneider
All rights reserved

Unless otherwise stated, all images are from the author's collection.

First published 2020

Manufactured in the United States

ISBN 9781467146616

Library of Congress Control Number: 2020934364

Notice: The information in this book is true and complete to the best of our knowledge. It is offered without guarantee on the part of the authors or The History Press. The authors and The History Press disclaim all liability in connection with the use of this book.

All rights reserved. No part of this book may be reproduced or transmitted in any form whatsoever without prior written permission from the publisher except in the case of brief quotations embodied in critical articles and reviews

If you can't explain it simply, you don't know it well enough.
—Albert Einstein

CONTENTS

CONTENTS

CONTENTS

CONTENTS

INTRODUCTION

Boats in the harbor are safe, but that is not what they are meant for.
—Zig Zigler

THE PERFECT GIFT

Just before my dad passed away at age ninety-four, he and my mom talked about my love of boating. They both knew I had been admiring a particular boat for sale but also realized I probably couldn't afford to buy it. So just days before we would say our last goodbye at a hospice in Florida, my dad whispered in my ear to say he wanted to buy me a boat. I was so grateful and would have eagerly traded his gift for any amount of extended time with him. I loved and respected my dad.

Today, a few years after his passing, his parting gift is where I spend a lot of time thinking about and enjoying life.

I named the boat *The Casalecki*, which is a word my dad made up and often used to describe something he thought was grandiose or magnificent. It's an appropriate name because being in my boat is a superb experience. It is very casalecki, as he might have said. After all, my boat is where I thought about writing a book about the history of Raritan Bay and the waterways that flow into it.

Over the years, I've been boating in Raritan Bay under many different circumstances. I've been serenely comforted by the calmness of the water's

surface as I watched a beautiful sunset. I've been distraught when I ran out of gas or my motor stopped for no apparent reason, and I had to wave to passersby for help. And I've also been terrified when I was in the middle of a horrific storm and thought my boat would sink. Thank goodness for members of the U.S. Coast Guard, who rescued me.

Raritan Bay is shaped like a triangular piece of pie. It's approximately nine miles long (east to west) and twelve miles wide (north to south) at its widest point, where it meets the Atlantic Ocean. There also are waterways that flow into Raritan Bay, such as Sandy Hook Bay and New York Harbor as well as the Shrewsbury and Raritan Rivers, Arthur Kill and the Navesink Estuary.

The history associated with Raritan Bay, and the waterways that fill it, is the focus of this book. Many of the historic events described in these pages are associated with the bays, rivers, creeks, harbors, marshes, ocean and so on. The water will be the common thread that weaves these stories about our past together. In many ways, our boat is positioned perfectly in Raritan Bay directly over an epicenter; the seismic waves of events from the past are radiating outward in all directions.

WHAT LIES BELOW

Below our boat is a murky and somewhat muddy bottom, much like history itself. Not everything we learn about our past is easy to find or always clear.

The rivers and streams provide fresh water while the Atlantic Ocean carries salt water into Raritan Bay with every incoming tide. As a result, we are floating where the water below us is brackish. Brackish water has a bit more salinity (salt) than fresh water but not as much salinity as seawater.

Marine life from the ocean, which thrives in salt water, will occasionally enter brackish water to look for food or sometimes because they are lost. These creatures may survive for a time, but usually, many of them feel much more comfortable in a saltwater environment. Unfortunately, some die from too much exposure to fresh water.

Whales, dolphins and seals are often seen in Raritan or Sandy Hook Bays feeding on the fish living here. It's not unusual to see whales breach next to boats as they try to scoop up a school of fish or to watch dolphins frolicking in the rivers, or even seals gathering on islands or rocks along the shoreline of Sandy Hook.

There are lots of fish to catch in Raritan Bay, such as fluke, winter flounder, bluefish, tautog and many more. And there are crabs, lobsters, mussels, clams and prehistoric-like crustaceans called horseshoe crabs, which may prove to outlive the diminishing population of oysters that once flourished in this bay. Today, many people find the fossilized remains of these species in places miles from water where the ancient seas once covered the more inland parts of New Jersey and New York.

Below our boat is the line of demarcation between New York and New Jersey, which was determined in 1884 by a commission representing both states. It's a reminder of the territorial rights claimed by the towns, states and counties below the surface of the water.

From our vantage point in the middle of the bay, the sun appears to rise and set on the water. It rises in the east on the horizon of the Atlantic Ocean and seems to set on the water in the western part of Raritan Bay. It's often a spectacular sight as boats full of people come out of nowhere to experience the beauty of the setting sun. And if there's a slight wind, the sailboats rush from their marinas on all sides to fill their sails.

If we threw out an anchor, it would drop about ten to thirty feet before reaching the bottom, which happens to be the average depth of the bay. In some places, the depth reaches more than one hundred feet, such as in the

New York and New Jersey Bight.

dredged channels where large ships enter the bay from the so-called New York–New Jersey Bight.

The bight is an underwater indentation along the eastern coast from Cape May Inlet in New Jersey to Montauk Point at the tip of Long Island. Our bight is mostly the continental shelf, which includes an underwater canyon (Hudson Canyon) formed by the Hudson River flowing through an ancient river valley during the ice ages, when the sea level was much lower. We'll talk more about the history of the creation of the bay a little later. Today, however, the bight includes all the major shipping channels that access New York Harbor and Arthur Kill.

INSIDE THE CIRCLE

To be clear, we're going to focus on the history of what's on, below and surrounding Raritan Bay. So imagine we are still floating in the middle of Raritan Bay, and there's an imaginary circle extending no more than 30 miles in all directions. The inside of this circle encompasses about 2,800 square miles of historical geography. For the most part, all of the history you'll read about in this book lies within the circle.

There is certainly an incredible number of historical events outside our circular boundary, but this book would then expand into a series of books if we attempted to write about it.

I cannot think of many other locations within our country that have hosted as many historical events as Raritan Bay and the surrounding region. Therefore, there are lots of stories to tell, and many of them will be told within these pages.

I know that not everybody likes history because it doesn't always lend itself to the kind of dramatic exposition that might have you leaning forward at the edge of your seat in eager anticipation of the next word or page or chapter. I like my history as simple as possible, so my writing style emphasizes the story. And when you look through the appropriate lens, the stories may become fascinating and even provocative.

So, before we begin looking for the stories within our defined territory, I'd like to review some of the waterways we'll explore as we go forward. However, if you're familiar with all of the waterways that flow into Raritan Bay, you may wish to skip over this section and go directly to the first chapter.

LAY OF THE WATER

Arthur Kill

I think Arthur Kill (also known as the Staten Island Sound) has always been the most interesting waterway. The name *Arthur Kill* is from the Dutch *achter kill*, which means "back channel." It's a tidal strait between Staten Island (a borough of New York City) and Union and Middlesex Counties in New Jersey. It is a primary navigational channel about ten miles long and runs south from the Port of New York and New Jersey to Raritan Bay.

Along the New Jersey side of the Arthur Kill are primarily industrial sites, part of which is called the Chemical Coast. Not quite an endearing moniker, but it has been the site of a few polluting spills in its history, so the name fits. The Staten Island side is lined with salt marshes, and they, too, are not entirely free of pollution.

Draining into the Arthur Kill is the Elizabeth River, which flows for some twelve miles through Essex and Union Counties in New Jersey. The Rahway River, Morses Creek and Piles Creek also enter Arthur Kill. The Passaic River joins the Hackensack River at the northern end of Newark Bay, which is a back bay of New York Harbor.

On the Staten Island side, Old Place Creek, Fresh Kills (fed by Richmond and Main Creeks), Bridge Creek (off Goethals Pond), Old Place Creek and Sawmill Creek flow into Arthur Kill.

The Saw Mill Creek area was a resource for the Lenape Native Americans as well as the early colonists. Both cultures harvested oysters from the creek and cultivated squash, corn and beans near the salt marshes where the creek flows into Arthur Kill.

Raritan River

Geologists believe the Raritan River was probably the major channel during the ice age that provided drainage from melting glaciers into what is now Raritan Bay. Today, the Raritan River flows for some twenty-three miles from its north branch, where it originates as a spring-fed stream in Morris County, New Jersey. Then it flows southward to its confluence at its South Branch, where it continues to flow another thirty-one miles until it reaches Raritan Bay. The waters of both the Raritan River and Arthur Kill come together off the shores of Perth Amboy, New Jersey.

From here, let's take our boat along the southern shore of Staten Island to New York Harbor, which is an estuary. And we have to be very careful as we enter this harbor because our relatively small boat will be overshadowed by giant cruise ships and freighters.

By the way, this will be the first time in our story we talk about tidal estuaries. So what are they? An estuary is any waterway with an almost direct connection to the ocean. The waterway is then affected every time water from the ocean enters and recedes during the rhythmic flow of the tides. The seawater entering the estuary is also diluted by the fresh water flowing from rivers and streams.

New York Harbor

The New York–New Jersey Harbor Estuary (also known as the Hudson-Raritan Estuary) is part of a complicated system of waterways and natural harbors. The depth of the navigational channels was deepened from the natural depth of seventeen feet centuries ago to at least forty-five feet today.

Sandy Hook Bay

A lot of folks think that Sandy Hook Bay is the large mouth of the Shrewsbury River, which empties into Raritan Bay. Others believe it to be part of the Raritan Bay, which also makes sense.

Let's start by defining the boundaries of Sandy Hook, which is a large sand peninsula or barrier spit extending from Sea Bright, New Jersey, to its terminus at the entrance to Raritan Bay from the Atlantic Ocean.

On the western edge of Sandy Hook is the Shrewsbury River, which flows into Sandy Hook Bay. The only towns on the shoreline of Sandy Hook Bay are Highlands and Atlantic Highlands, New Jersey. Drawing an imaginary line from the tip of Sandy Hook westerly toward Atlantic Highlands would be the dividing line between Sandy Hook Bay and Raritan Bay. This particular area is beloved by clammers (or diggers) who rake for clams.

Shrewsbury River

The Shrewsbury River is approximately eight miles long and extends from Oceanport to its confluence with the Navesink estuary and then north in a narrow channel to Sandy Hook Bay at Highlands.

Today, the Shrewsbury River is protected from the open Atlantic Ocean on its eastern side by a long barrier peninsula that extends north to become Sandy Hook. Two resort-oriented towns on the peninsula include Monmouth Beach and Sea Bright.

However, during the 1700s and 1800s, there were openings (or breaks) in Sandy Hook, which allowed boats to travel directly from the Shrewsbury River to the Atlantic Ocean. As a result, Oceanport became a major port for ships that could travel down the Shrewsbury River and enter the ocean through one of the breaks in Sandy Hook and then travel directly north to the New York Harbor with loads of goods.

The merchants and ship owners in Oceanport were competing with other ports, such as Keyport and Port Monmouth, New Jersey, until the channel openings in Sandy Hook closed up over time and there was no longer any faster route to New York City.

Navesink Estuary

The Navesink River is an estuary approximately eight miles long and is surrounded by the communities of Middletown, Red Bank, Fair Haven and Rumson. Known officially as the North Shrewsbury River, and upstream of Red Bank as the Swimming River with several smaller streams, it eventually connects to the Shrewsbury River at Rumson.

So there you have it. The waterways and bays outlined here are all an integral part of the stories of our past. Almost every decade or century has had its connection to these watery trails through time.

1

THE BEGINNING

THE PREHISTORIC PAST

What is history? An echo of the past in the future; a reflex from the future on the past.

—*Victor Hugo*

My love of natural history began on some railroad tracks in Florida, where I lived as a boy. I can still remember the smell of creosote, which was used to treat wooden railroad ties. And I was always fascinated by those rusted railroad spikes that had been tossed aside for me to pick up and bring home as souvenirs.

What piqued my curiosity, however, were calcified crystals imbedded in a rock called coquina, which is a soft limestone made of broken shells. It was often used in road making in the Caribbean and Florida. And I was fascinated by this combination of yellow crystals and actual shells or fossils in a rock. Whenever I found one of these rocks, it was like finding treasure.

This fascination with rocks, fossils and crystals was the beginning of my interest in how the world was formed. It was so exciting to me, I eventually graduated from George Washington University with a degree in both geophysics (geology) and journalism. My intention in obtaining these two degrees was to be able to write about the history of the earth. And so I am.

The study of the origin of our universe some 13 billion (13,000,000,000) years ago, and when Earth was formed about 4 billion years ago, always fascinated me. Even contemplating such a vastness of time boggles my mind.

To think, a fossil of a winged reptile that lived 200 million years ago was found in 1961 entombed in black shale within a quarry in New Jersey. The fossil was then sold at an auction in the year 2000 for $167,500 and donated to the American Museum of Natural History in New York City. My fossil collection pales in comparison.

THE BIG ONES GOT AWAY

Dinosaurs are extinct today because they lacked opposable thumbs and the brainpower to build a space program.

—*Neil deGrasse Tyson*

Who doesn't love dinosaurs? They almost seem mythological, but we know they existed. We've seen their fossilized skeletons in the Museum of Natural History. Still, it's hard to believe they roamed our earth.

One of the most interesting prehistoric periods when dinosaurs flourished was from 65 to 135 million years ago, when lots of activities were taking place. The Cretaceous period was when creatures began their evolution toward looking a lot like our modern mammals, birds and insects.

During the early Cretaceous, the continents were also in very different positions than they are today. There was one so-called supercontinent called Pangaea, and it was slowly torn apart. As a result, the separate continents (as we generally know them today) started drifting into position.

By the middle of this period, ocean levels were a lot higher, and most of the land was underwater. By the end of the Cretaceous period, the continents were much closer to the positions they're in today.

Many of today's florists are also fans of this period because it's when flowering plants began developing. Coincidentally, pollinating insects, like bees and wasps, evolved just prior to welcoming the flowers.

During the Cretaceous period, more birds began taking flight. The first bird to develop a beak was about the size of a crow.

Both New Jersey and New York, as well as many states along the Eastern Seaboard, contain fossilized remains of several late Cretaceous-era dinosaurs and reptiles along a stretch of what used to be a shallow ocean.

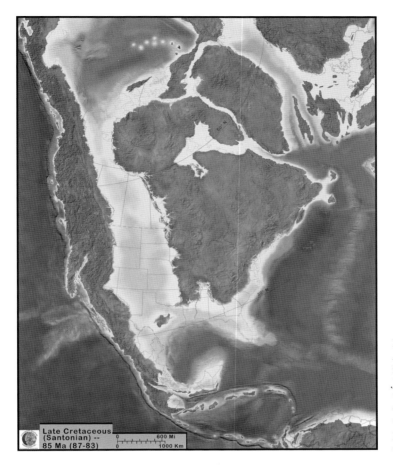

Most of North America, including New Jersey, was underwater during the Cretaceous period. *Courtesy of USGS.*

Fortunately, the green sand, or marl, found along this stretch of shallow water was perfect for preserving fossils such as cow sharks—descendants of which still exist today.

We also find the fossilized remains of the dreaded mosasaurus, a fifty-foot extinct carnivorous aquatic lizard that looked like a cross between a shark and an alligator. I wouldn't want to meet one of these creatures.

The most famous discovery of a fossil within the coastal plain sediment in our area was a duck-billed dinosaur known as a hadrosaurus. It was discovered in Haddonfield, New Jersey, in 1835 and became the very first complete dinosaur skeleton to be found in America. The hadrosaurus was a vegetarian, grew to ten feet tall and was very peaceful, fortunately. Incidentally, the Monmouth Museum has a replica of the skull of a hadrosaur, which is also the official state dinosaur of New Jersey.

Left: The mosasaurus lived in Raritan Bay during the Cretaceous period. *Courtesy National Geographic.*

Below: The hadrosaurus roamed the shoreline of Raritan Bay.

Oh, by the way, the fossilized remains of the diatryma, a seven-foot-tall flightless bird that may have been carnivorous, have been found in New Jersey and New York. It looked a lot like the dodo, another flightless bird, which became extinct in 1681.

THE SKY IS FALLING

The story of Henny-Penny has the best opening in all literature: "The sky is falling, cried Henny-Penny, and a piece of it fell on my tail."
—*John Steinbeck*

No one was there to see it happen, but suddenly the dinosaurs had left the building. Scientists all over the world started examining a layer of sediment that was laid down some sixty-five million years ago when dinosaurs were last seen. It was a grayish layer and contained high concentrations of iridium, an element that is rare on Earth but common in most meteorites. While that's very interesting, they also found tektites, which form when rock is suddenly vaporized then immediately cooled. You don't have to be a geologist to figure out what happened. An extraterrestrial object struck Earth with great force. Ouch!

And to prove it, there happens to be a massive impact crater on the Yucatán Peninsula that dates precisely to this time. The Yucatán Peninsula separates the Gulf of Mexico from the Caribbean Sea, encompassing parts of Mexico, Belize and Guatemala. The crater site is more than one hundred miles in diameter. A chemical analysis shows that the sedimentary rock of the area was melted and mixed by extremely high temperatures similar to the blast impact of an asteroid six miles in diameter.

It seems the asteroid collided with Earth and sent shockwaves, massive tsunamis and a vast cloud of hot rock and dust into the atmosphere. The debris rose into the atmosphere and eventually fell on those poor creatures and cooked the dinosaurs alive. Yikes. Poor dinosaurs. They never knew what hit them. They must have tasted like chicken. But don't worry about all of the cute and cuddly animals because they could burrow and hide during the torrential downpour of debris from the atmosphere.

A supplemental theory states a cloud of dust stayed in the atmosphere and blocked the sun's rays for months or even years. With less sunlight, plants and the animals dependent on them would have died as well.

ROLLERCOASTER OF WEATHER

In the spring, I have counted 136 different kinds of weather inside of 24 hours.
—Mark Twain

And what's all of this talk about extinction have to do with Raritan Bay?

Well, we were still experiencing high sea levels in our area. And with the dinosaurs gone, for whatever reason, marine life, including sea snails, fish, sharks and burrowing shrimp, started to thrive.

The highest sea level we ever reached in our area was fifteen million years ago. It was quite warm in those days. There was very little ice at the poles, and we didn't see much snow. It must have seemed like a tropical paradise all over the earth.

We know the sea level was high because of the extensive amount of marine sand and associated gravel deposits found on many of the highest hills throughout the region, such as the gravel of Beacon Hill located in Marlboro Township, New Jersey. Incidentally, the hill was so named because it was a lookout point that oversaw Raritan Bay and the presence of British troops could be reported.

The sea levels would fluctuate during the next twelve million years. After all the dizzying up and down of sea levels, it started getting cold from two million to twenty thousand years ago. As all of the land creatures began getting dressed for colder weather, the sea level started to drop significantly. Why? You probably guessed correctly. Significant quantities of water were being frozen, which resulted in enormous glaciers that were moving at a snail's pace and headed toward our area. Once in a while, it would warm up again, and the glaciers would melt a bit and appear to recede. Mostly, however, the glaciers advanced more than they retreated.

This was not a great place to live while everything was completely frozen. No animals, no humans. Most of us probably headed southwest to escape the cold.

At one point in history, much of the northern part of our hemisphere was covered in one extensive sheet of ice. It was the dreaded Laurentide Ice Sheet, which covered millions of square miles, including most of Canada and a large portion of the northern United States. Its forward-moving front was heading south toward our neck of the woods, and it was taking its sweet time getting here. It was getting colder all the time now, but nobody worried because they had time to get out of here before turning into popsicles.

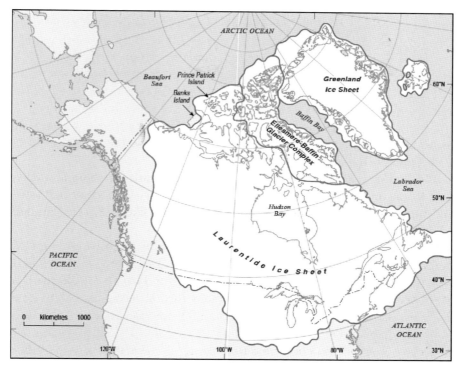

The Laurentide Ice Sheet covered most of North America.

If the Laurentide Ice Sheet was the parent, then several glaciers were the children who were usually close at hand. One of the kids, however, decided to venture out ahead of its parent. The Wisconsin Glacier finally arrived in our area and decided to stay awhile in today's New York City, Staten Island and northern New Jersey. What a bummer! As soon as this kid arrived, it started causing trouble. First, its ice was so thick and so heavy at the Verrazano Narrows it prevented the Hudson River from flowing into the sea. As a result, the Hudson River was diverted westward to carve out today's Kill van Kull (above Staten Island) and subsequently the Arthur Kill that headed south to the Raritan River Valley.

It's also important to note one characteristic of almost all glaciers. Just like kids, they like to scoop up everything in their path, such as boulders, stones, gravel and sand, and drag it along with them. They'll keep doing this until they stop moving. By the time the Wisconsin Glacier stopped at the southern end of Staten Island, it was full of those stones, gravel and sand. When the weather got warm and the glaciers began defrosting and then melting, they appear to recede. As they do, everything they carry during their journey gets dropped right where it was. Usually, the stones clump together as the ice melts. The clump is finally revealed when the ice has completely melted. Geologists call these mounds of rock and gravel glacial moraines.

From the vantage point of our boat in Raritan Bay, we can see hills on the southern end of Staten Island that were part of the southern terminal moraine formed by the Wisconsin Glacier, which finally started receding ten thousand years ago.

And also remember that the sea level was extremely low while the glacier was visiting our area because most of the water was frozen. As a result, the beaches along the Atlantic Ocean were, in some cases, almost two miles farther out than they are today. Raritan Bay didn't exist. Well, it existed, but as a river valley.

The Raritan River was a slow, winding river that flowed through the valley and then out to sea, which was much farther out. It was very different than today. Our boat would have been floating in a meandering river.

While the dinosaurs bit the dust much earlier, mastodons (like giant hairy elephants with huge curved tusks) were roaming throughout our area. According to geologic researchers, the mastodon was the most abundant and largest of all the creatures wandering through the Raritan River Valley. Since 1800, more than fifty fossils have been found in New Jersey. Incidentally, the mastodon was similar to the wooly mammoth but shorter

Mastodons, also known as wooly mammoths, were prevalent in the Raritan River Valley. *Courtesy of New York State Museum.*

and a bit stockier in build. Scientists believe mastodons were here from ten to thirteen thousand years ago, when the Wisconsin Glacier was receding.

Scientists also believe the mastodons were probably trapped in soft mud at the edge of the glacier and subsequently drowned and were eventually fossilized. Several fossilized remains have also been found off the coast of New Jersey from a period when the sea level was much lower.

The Geology Museum at Rutgers has a full skeleton on display; it is the only complete skeleton found in New Jersey. The partial remains of a mastodon were discovered in Holmdel during 2013.

WATER, WATER, EVERYWHERE

"We're gonna live!" [Water rapidly rises around them.] *"We're gonna die!"*

—*Sid, in the movie* Ice Age: The Meltdown

As the ice started melting, it was good enough for us humans and other animals to start moving back to this beautiful area. We didn't know at the time our peaceful valley was slowly filling with water. It was filling so slowly we hardly noticed.

As it started getting warmer, many of the coastal regions were resettled by people who were accustomed to village-style living in tidewater communities that subsisted on hunting and gathering marine shellfish and, eventually, on agriculture. A group of others enjoyed living in the valley along the river. They had no idea they'd be underwater within a few thousand years—poor planning on their part.

During our local glacial meltdown, huge amounts of sediment from the Raritan River were filling in the valley faster than the sea level could flood the shorelines. Portions of the valley that were once exposed several thousands of years ago were now being buried under 150 feet of mud. The mud, however, helped develop some of the tidal wetlands and marshes along the south and west ends of Raritan Bay, including the wetlands in Cheesequake State Park. Incidentally, it's interesting to note that sand covers the sea bottom in the lower portion of the bay, while mud is mostly located at the bottom in the middle part of Raritan Bay.

While you know about the bluffs created by moraines on the southern end of Staten Island, the hills of the Highlands of Navesink were composed of

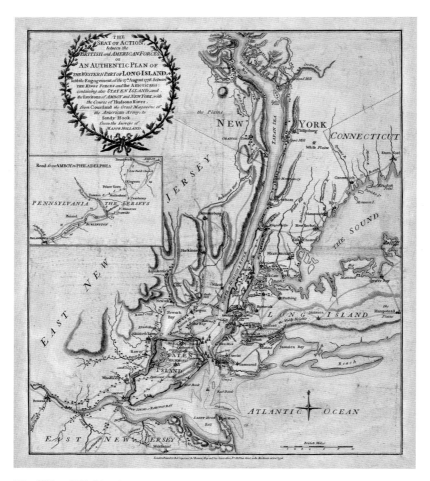

The Hills of Highlands.

uplifted layers of hardened sands, mud and gravel from the Atlantic Coastal Plain. The uplift of these hills is attributed to glacial rebound, although it is possible that other geologic processes were occurring. Post-glacial rebound is when the land rises after the massive weight of an ice sheet no longer exerts pressure on the bedrock below. It's quite natural.

The Highlands of Navesink are a range of low hills with an upland area reaching more than 350 feet in elevation. Crawford Hill, at an elevation of 391 feet, is the highest point in Monmouth County, New Jersey.

The seaward front of the Highlands of Navesink constitutes the highest point along the coast of New Jersey, which reaches an elevation of 266 feet at Mount Mitchell. Across Raritan Bay, Staten Island's highest point south of Maine, but still along the Eastern Seaboard, is Todt Hill, which reaches 406 feet.

The topmost geologic layer of the Highlands of Navesink is composed of sand, gravel and erosion-resistant ironstone, which is a layer located on the highest summits of the hills in our area. This layer protects the more easily weathered underlying geologic layers, such as the well-known Navesink Formation.

While the glaciers continued melting, the resulting water started flooding the valleys of the Hudson and Raritan Rivers and the Arthur Kill. During this period of warming, the area surrounding the Raritan River Valley transformed from tundra to forests of spruce and pine. Before long, the forests became deciduous.

When Raritan Bay began filling up with water about 2,500 years ago, the sea level was rising about a foot every hundred years. In geologic time, it was like the speed of lightning. If we were in our boat, we would start rising as the valley began filling. Many believe the Raritan River was the principal channel along the front of the glacier, which drained the water from the melting ice. As Raritan Bay began to fill, large oyster beds began forming along the tributaries.

By the 1600s, oysters grew in two large beds in the western end of the bay. The largest measured oyster bed was about a mile across and was located just beyond the mouth of the Raritan River. The beds were contiguous with oysters that were lining the Raritan River estuary for as much as five miles upstream.

Oysters also grew abundantly along the other tributary rivers of Raritan Bay, including the East, Hudson, Navesink and Shrewsbury Rivers, as well as along most of the Arthur Kill and in southern portions of Newark Bay. A smaller oyster colony, called the Chingarora bed, was located in what became Keyport Harbor.

2

THE NATIVES

THE RETURNING NATIVES

When you know who you are; when your mission is clear, and you burn with the inner fire of unbreakable will; no cold can touch your heart; no deluge can dampen your purpose. You know that you are alive.
—Chief Seattle, Duwamish (1780–1866)

As the area surrounding Raritan Bay began to get warmer, the first people who started moving into it were the Lenape Indians. Lenape, meaning "true men" or "standard men," began to establish villages along the bay and next to the rivers running into the bay.

Suffice it to say, there were lots and lots of people living in America long before any Europeans, or anyone else for that matter, set foot on this continent. In New York and New Jersey, the Delaware Indians were prevalent and closely associated with the Algonquian tribes.

And while the great numbers of these natives have diminished dramatically, almost to the point of extinction, much of their language has carried on in the names of towns, roads and rivers. Raritan Bay, for example, is named after the Raritans, a branch of the Lenape tribe.

The Delaware Nation occupied all of the state of New Jersey, the western end of Long Island, all of Staten and Manhattan Islands and neighboring parts of the mainland, along with other portions of New York west of

Lenape Indian chief painting
by Gustavus Hesselius (1838).

the Hudson, parts of eastern Pennsylvania and northern Delaware. There
were hundreds, if not thousands, of villages throughout New York and
New Jersey.

There were three major divisions: the Munsee in northern New Jersey
and adjacent portions of New York west of the Hudson; the Unalachtigo in
northern Delaware, southeastern Pennsylvania and southern New Jersey;
and the Unami in the intermediate territory, extending to the western end
of Long Island.

They began establishing a way to trade and exchange food and goods.
And while other tribes in the area ridiculed them because of their
nonaggressive nature, they would very often act as facilitators in resolving
conflicts between other tribes.

Some Lenape lived in small groups of fifty to one hundred people, while
others lived in larger groups of several hundred in villages along the banks
of rivers. They hunted and fished. They also farmed and gathered wild
plants, seeds and nuts. They lived in traditional wigwams, which were built
with saplings and covered with bark or cattail mats. Several families could
live together and occupy larger dwellings called longhouses.

The men cleared the land, built houses to live in and constructed canoes. They also fished, hunted and traded with other tribes or villages. The women planted crops, collected firewood, prepared animal hides and also made clothing. They were responsible for gathering the ingredients for the meals they would prepare. They also did most of the parenting of their children, who were expected to share the workload.

The early explorers and settlers who first saw the Lenape described them as tall, well-built natives with muscular physiques. They were also quick on their feet and could endure long journeys.

Typically, men wore loincloths, but when it became colder, cloaks of fur with leggings and soft moccasins would be worn. Women wore wraparound skirts and, in colder weather, poncho-like tops called a yoke. Beautiful robes were also created from goose or turkey feathers carefully sewn into some netting. Often, their clothes were painted, fringed or decorated with shell beads or porcupine quills. Ornaments were also made from stones, bones or antlers, shells or animal claws.

LIVING AND DYING

The Great Spirit is in all things, he is in the air we breathe. The Great Spirit is our Father, but the Earth is our Mother. She nourishes us, that which we put into the ground she returns to us.
—*Big Thunder of the Algonquins*

The Lenape believed in a creator called Kishelemukong (He who creates with his thoughts). He was the all-powerful entity that created all good things, including the Manetuwak, which were the spirit helpers who lived in and controlled the forces of nature, plants and animals. Mahtantu, however, was an evil spirit who created irritating insects and harmful plants and put sharp thorns on bushes. Bad stuff.

The Lenape believed all living things had spirits, even plants, rocks and the air they breathed. So, it stood to reason that everything was to be respected. Every member of the tribe tried to live in harmony with everything surrounding them.

The Lenape enjoyed being clean and frequently took steam baths in a sweat lodge to purify themselves. They all knew how to use plants to cure sickness or injuries. They would often consult a particular doctor depending on their ailment. For example, the Nentpikes knew how to apply natural remedies, such as herbs. The Meteinu or Medew would be consulted when the Lenape required help from the spirit world.

The death of anyone was always considered to be very tragic. The memorial service and subsequent burial were always a celebration of life; the departed was dressed in new clothes and interred in a shallow grave. The soul of the deceased would make its journey to the afterlife where Kishelemukong was waiting.

GLORIOUS OYSTERS

A hungry stomach makes a short prayer.

—Native American proverb

The Lenape loved oysters. They may not have lived where the oysters and clams were located, but they certainly traveled during the summer to live at the water's edge to feast on them.

When summer was over, they moved back to their more permanent villages to plant crops for the spring, which could then be harvested in the fall. During winter months, they hunted in the wooded areas. How do we know? There are telltale middens located all around us. And by the way, middens are not something children wear on their hands to keep warm in the winter. Ha, ha.

A midden is nothing more than an old garbage dump and may include animal bones, human excrement, botanical material, mollusk shells or any other artifacts associated with human habitat. Some middens are hundreds of feet long, consisting of thousands of clam and oyster shells pressed together along with shards of bones and broken pottery. In 1839, a journalist described middens as plentiful and "bleached white as snow."

The Lenape ate clams and oysters regularly, as did their ancestors, chucking the shells into enormous piles over thousands of years. For example, a whole bunch of large middens have been found around Raritan Bay and on Staten Island, which is a testament to the Lenape's reliance on Raritan Bay for food.

There were once so many oyster middens in New York City that much of the city was built on top of them. The Glidden Midden of Maine is the largest in the northeastern states, but it doesn't compare to the size of its neighbor, the Whaleback Midden, which was 1,650 feet in length and more than 1,320 feet wide. And like many of the middens during the 1800s, the contents of it were mostly used to make mortar and supplement chicken feed. Ancient shells were also used in place of rocks to build foundations for new railway and road systems. Also, the Hudson Railroad and Metro-North lines of New York ran over and through dozens of middens.

Thank goodness it's illegal today to disturb an oyster midden without permission. Today, when archaeologists excavate a midden, they are meticulous in recording the location and description of every item in the pile.

For example, during the restoration of the Statue of Liberty during the 1980s, an oyster midden was found on Liberty Island. More than nine thousand artifacts, such as ancient tools, bones, broken pottery and refuse, were recovered. Arrowheads, stone axes, ceramics and other objects left here long ago by the Lenape and their ancestors are still occasionally found in farmers' fields or along riverbanks.

3

THE EXPLORERS

WHO'S ON FIRST?

O brave new world that has such people in it.

—Aldous Huxley

Nearly five hundred years before the birth of Christopher Columbus, a group of European explorers was searching for a new world and discovered North America. So, while Columbus is honored with a federal holiday every year, the man considered by many to be the leader of the first European expedition to North America was Leif Eriksson, a Viking. As far as we know, however, he didn't make it into Raritan Bay.

Then there's Columbus, who completed four round-trip voyages (1492 to 1503) between Spain and the Americas. These voyages were the beginning of serious European exploration and then eventually colonization of all the American continents. He didn't enter Raritan Bay, either.

Then along came Italian explorer John Cabot, who discovered the coast of North America in 1497 for Henry VII of England. Cabot became the earliest known European explorer of coastal North America since the Vikings during the eleventh century. He came close to Raritan Bay but receives no cigar for his effort.

By 1507, a new world map was drawn by Martin Waldseemüller, who named the continent of the New World *America* in honor of Amerigo

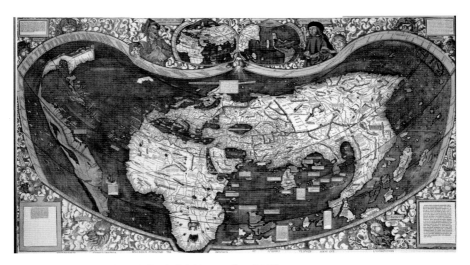

First map of the world by Martin Waldseemüller (1507).

Vespucci, an Italian explorer, financier, navigator and cartographer who mostly explored South America.

Another explorer, Ponce de León, explored the coast of Florida in 1513, looking for the Fountain of Youth. There were three ships with two hundred men on this expedition. I grew up in Florida and was invited to drink water bubbling from a spring supposed to be the actual Fountain of Youth. Nope. It was a fraud. I have become older with time.

Finally, in 1524, the real deal came to visit us. Italian explorer Giovanni Da Verrazano left Madeira, a region of Portugal, and eventually entered New York Harbor during a French expedition from the Carolinas to Nova Scotia. This voyage is considered to be the first European exploration of the Atlantic Seaboard of North America since the Viking expeditions five hundred years earlier. Verrazano explored the coast of New Jersey and called it Lorraine.

To him and his crew, this was a land mainly comprising a vast expanse of water in Raritan Bay, marshes, swamps, forests and hills. He wrote about the local natives: they were "clothed in feathers of birds of various colours"; he also described "a small mountain which stands by the sea." Many believe this is the "mountain" on which the Twin Lights of Navesink now stands, or perhaps it was Todt Hill on Staten Island.

Incidentally, a century later, after Da Verrazano named the area Lorraine, the Swedes called it New Sweden and the Dutch subsequently called it New

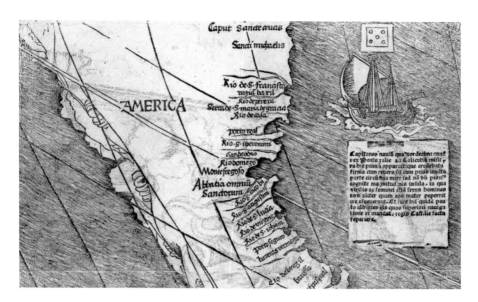

Above: Closeup of America (1507).

Left: Explorer Giovanni Da Verrazano.

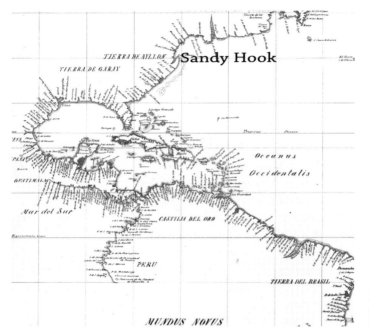

Diego Ribero draws Sandy Hook on map.

Netherland. The name *New Jersey* appeared for the first time in a royal grant issued by King Charles II's brother, James, Duke of York, in 1664.

After Verrazano, there arrived several other explorers who came to map this new world so others could make their way across the ocean to explore it for themselves.

Maps were being drawn left and right. One significant map was drawn by Spaniard Diego Ribero, who created the first known map in 1529 of the East Coast of America, showing details of Sandy Hook, then called Cabo de Arenas or "Cape of Sands."

A little more than twenty-five years after Da Verrazano described the Lenape natives, the government of Spain wanted in on the action. In 1550, a debate over the treatment and status of Indians in the New World was held where it was proposed the American Indians should be considered free men who deserve equal treatment to European colonists. The opposing argument stated the local Indians should be considered as slaves.

Meanwhile, England successfully battled the Spanish Armada in 1588, which lessened Spain's influence in the New World and increased England's influence in the Americas.

Everybody wanted a piece of the action in the New World. Casinos? Resorts? The sky might be the limit!

ENTER THE *HALF MOON*

These natives are a very good people; for when they saw that I would not remain, they supposed that I was afraid of their bows; and, taking their arrows, they broke them in pieces and threw them into the fire.

—Henry Hudson

One of the world's most famous explorers in our area was Henry Hudson. He was mostly consumed with looking for different trade routes to Asia, but he never accomplished this particular goal. Instead, he became instrumental in the settlement of our specific part of the world.

Hudson had joined the Dutch East India Company to command a ship that would cross the Atlantic Ocean toward what is now called Nova Scotia. From there, Hudson sailed south along the coast of North America until he reached Chesapeake Bay. It was there he made a U-turn and headed back toward New York Harbor, which he knew had been discovered by Verrazano more than eighty years earlier.

Then, in 1609, Hudson sailed into Raritan Bay on a ship called the *Half Moon* for the very first time. One of Hudson's crew members described the land surrounding Raritan Bay. "It is a very good land to fall in with, and a pleasant land to see," recorded First Mate Robert Juet. He also wrote, "At three of the clock in the afternoon we came to three great rivers."

Historians have debated precisely where the *Half Moon* was initially anchored. The three great rivers may have been the Shrewsbury River, the Narrows (which generally separates New York Harbor from Raritan Bay) and Rockaway Inlet, which is a strait connecting Jamaica Bay with Raritan Bay.

Regardless of his exact position, Hudson moored his ship in Raritan Bay or possibly Sandy Hook Bay, and within a short period of time, he was socializing with the Lenape natives. In fact, the natives were quite nice and dressed in colorful clothes. During the initial encounters, Hudson tasted his first mouthful of the local corn, which he called "Turkish wheat."

Many of Hudson's crew members went ashore to spend time with the

English explorer Henry Hudson.

Lenape, who gave their new visitors gifts of tobacco. In an exchange, to symbolize friendship, Hudson gave them knives and beads. He described the encounter in his diary and called them "very civil." While Hudson seemed to trust them, a few of the crew members did not. "Though we rode quietly at anchor, we did not trust them," one of the seamen wrote.

Hudson soon sent John Colman and four others to determine the depth of a river some twelve miles away, which could have been either the Raritan, Hudson or East River. Some historians claimed the five crew members went searching for fresh water in the hills of today's Atlantic Highlands, New Jersey. There's even a place called Henry Hudson's spring that has dripped contaminated water from a pipe stuck into the bedrock for many years. Unfortunately, regardless of their exact mission, some of the crew were attacked by natives who approached silently in two canoes. It was reported that more than two dozen natives were in the canoes.

Colman was a trusted crew member who had been with Hudson on an earlier voyage. Unfortunately, Colman was killed by an arrow through his neck during the attack. Two others were seriously wounded. Colman became the very first European to be murdered in the New World.

American poet Thomas Frost wrote "The Death of Colman":

> *Then prone he fell within the boat,*
> *A flinthead arrow through his throat*
> *And now full many a stealthy skiff*
> *Shot out into the bay;*
> *And swiftly, sadly, pulled we back*
> *To where the Half Moon lay;*
> *But he was dead our master wept*
> *He smiled, brave heart, as though he slept.*

The remaining crew members got away with their lives and made it back to the ship. The crew kept a careful watch after the unprovoked attack by the Lenape. The next day, Colman was buried ashore in a place they affectionately named Colman's Point, which today is the name of a point next to the pier in Keansburg, New Jersey.

Strangely, Hudson did not overreact or try to retaliate against the Lenape. Instead, he and his crew continued trading with the natives on board their ship. According to the ship's journal, the crew was watching and listening carefully to see if the natives made any mention of the men they attacked. No clues were ever provided.

HENRY HUDSON DESCENDING THE HUDSON RIVER.

Sir Henry Hudson meets with the Lenape on the banks of Raritan Bay.

However, one incident was recorded; it could have been disastrous if not for their already suspicious outlook. The ship's log reports that two "great canoes full of natives came on board in an attempt to deceive us, pretended interest in buying knives. But we were aware of their intent and took two of them, prisoners." The crew did so as insurance against any further attack.

Hudson wrote later: "Had they indicated by a cunning light in their eyes that they had knowledge of the foul murder, I was prepared to order my company to exterminate all without delay."

As fear began spreading throughout Hudson's ship, it became clear the explorers had worn out their welcome in Raritan Bay. They raised the anchor, and off they went through the Narrows and into New York Bay, where they lay anchor just off the southern tip of Manhattan. At the time, some of the Lenape were living on an island they called Mannahatta, meaning "Island of Many Hills."

Unfortunately, when it rained, it poured, as more than two dozen canoes filled with Lenape men, women and children began approaching the ship. One of the crew reported that they saw "the intent of their treachery and would not allow any of them to come aboard." Nevertheless, the crew traded for oysters. During the transactions, Hudson noticed the natives used copper in their smoking pipes and inferred there could be a natural source nearby.

Incidentally, the mining industry of New Jersey dates to the 1600s, when copper was first mined by Dutch settlers along the Delaware River in Warren County. One of the first iron mines in the United States was located in Morris County. Copper was prevalent in New Jersey, and the Lenape knew where to find it and how to use it. Today, there are some 450 underground mines in New Jersey, all now abandoned.

Hudson ordered the anchor to be pulled and headed farther north on his soon-to-be namesake river.

The *Half Moon* continued upriver, and Hudson once again encountered Lenape Indians. This time, Hudson accepted an invitation to dine with the chief of a local tribe. After feasting as the guest of honor, Hudson was to stay overnight but was fearful of accepting. The natives sensed his fear, so they broke their arrows and threw them in the fire to indicate their intentions. Regardless of this sign of good faith, Hudson returned to the ship.

Unfortunately, the *Half Moon* could go no farther north because the river had become too shallow. In fact, the ship ran aground a few times, so the crew turned back toward Raritan Bay.

Aboard the *Half Moon*, Hudson had explored the Hudson River as far up as today's Albany, New York. Along the way, Hudson noticed that the lush land lining the river contained lots of wildlife, and he wrote, "The land is the finest for cultivation that I ever in my life set foot upon."

As a footnote, on his way back to the Netherlands, Hudson was stopped in the English port of Dartmouth, where his ship was seized. Apparently, the English authorities were upset about Hudson exploring for another country and admonished him for working with the Dutch. Despite his reprimand, Hudson was passionate about finding the Northwest Passage and soon found English investors to fund his next journey. His final voyage would prove to be fatal.

4

THE TRADERS

ENTER THE DUTCH

You can never cross the ocean until you have the courage to lose sight of the shore.
—Dutch proverb

During the early 1600s, it took at least two months to cross the Atlantic Ocean from England to America. Utilizing the knowledge of explorers like Hudson, the Dutch made their way to the New World and started claiming parts of present-day New York and New Jersey for a new colony they called New Netherland.

The Dutch loved to trade, so many small trading colonies were developed where today's Jersey City and Hoboken are located. European glass beads and bottles, iron axes, knives, tools, brass kettles and ornaments of metal, cloth and clothing were cherished by the Lenape, which the Dutch would trade for pelts of bear, beaver, otter and deer.

Now that the New World was becoming the place to go, Dutch captain Adriaen Block undertook four voyages to the Northeast between 1611 and 1613 to establish fur trading with the Lenape. He was also charting the coastal waters and rivers of the region, which Henry Hudson had surveyed for the Dutch just a few years earlier.

While wintering in New York Bay during 1613, his ship caught fire and burned to the waterline. Working through the frigid winter, Block built a new

Replica of the *Onrust. Courtesy of the Navesink Maritime Heritage Association.*

boat in 1614 from the salvaged remnants and named it the *Onrust*, Dutch for "Unrest" or "Restlessness." It was the first vessel built by Europeans in New York State and was the first yacht to be built in the New World.

The same year, Block established the first fur trading post, Fort Nassau, in the current site of Albany, New York, which formed the basis for the first permanent European settlement in the Hudson Valley. Block named the area—extending from Pennsylvania into current New England—New Netherland and named Block Island after himself.

As an aside, a replica of the *Onrust* recently came into Raritan Bay, and I was provided an opportunity to climb on board and take pictures of the experience.

Then in 1624, another group of thirty French-speaking Protestant families from present-day Belgium decided to come here to avoid oppression. Some of these folks chose to settle on Governors Island, located at the mouth of the Hudson River. This is where they built a fort, a windmill and a few other structures. The settlers developed so quickly they had built themselves off the island and had to move by 1626. So they decided to relocate to the southern tip of the nearby Manhattan Island, which they called New Amsterdam. When other families learned about the new settlement, they moved to New Amsterdam as well.

Pretty soon, the place was jumping with Dutch settlers, not just the Dutch but lots of others from many other countries. Technically, the Dutch, Finnish and Swedish colonists were considered to be the first Europeans in New Jersey. Talk about diversity!

Meanwhile, the English settlements being built in New England were extremely homogeneous, in sharp contrast to what the Dutch were building.

The Dutch welcomed almost everyone: Africans (free and slave), Scots, English, Germans, Scandinavians, French Huguenots, Muslims, Jews and Native Americans. They all roamed the streets and seemed to enjoy one another's company for the most part. There were times, however, when ethnic rivalry got the better of people. For example, Peter Stuyvesant, the director-general of New Netherland, tried to prevent Jewish refugees from leaving their boat. He called them "very repugnant" and "deceitful." He wasn't such a nice guy and frequently persecuted Lutherans and Quakers. He also owned a whole bunch of slaves. Believe it or not, however, New Amsterdam was more tolerant than some other European colonies.

Nevertheless, the Dutch traders were not so kind to the Lenape and had little respect for these Native Americans. Some historians say some of the Dutch considered enslaving them but never did. Regardless of their feelings for Native Americans, the Dutch traded rum and guns for furs from the Lenape. Much of the trading took place in Pavonia, which was the first European settlement on the west bank of the North River (Hudson River). It was part of the seventeenth-century province of New Netherland in what would become the present Hudson County, New Jersey.

The relationship between the Dutch and the Lenape was tenuous, so trading agreements were often misunderstood. This led to several incidents, which only increased tensions. Eventually, in 1643, for whatever reasons, the head of the Dutch settlement ordered his soldiers to murder more than one hundred Indians, including women and children. It was a massacre. The Lenape called it "The Slaughter of the Innocents."

This attack united the Algonquian tribes like never before. As a result, eleven tribes of the Iroquois Nation retaliated in attacks on the local traders and settlers who were located from the Raritan River to the Connecticut River, which emptied into Long Island Sound. Over the next two years, settlers were continually harassed and killed randomly. In all, more than 1,600 natives were killed by the Dutch. Finally, a truce was reached in 1645.

A decade later, however, one of the Dutch settlers murdered a young Indian girl who was retrieving a pear from a tree. The violence started all over as the Lenape spent three days of retaliation with deadly attacks against the local settlers. They also burned settlements, kidnapped settlers and then demanded ransoms for their release.

Around 1660, some nine thousand people lived in New Netherland, and there wasn't much infrastructure to defend the population, which left it somewhat vulnerable should the English attack. It's important to remember that the English had fought three wars against the Dutch. They considered the Dutch their primary trading rivals between 1652 and 1674.

The Dutch loved to trade in and around Raritan Bay as well as in many of the connecting waterways. They were quite good at trading. Too much of a good thing, however, and the British would take notice and not in a good way.

By 1664, King Charles II of England had awarded the colony's land to his brother, the Duke of York, even though the English and the Dutch were not fighting with each other at the time. That changed dramatically when the Dutch woke up to find four British warships with several hundred soldiers at their front door in New Amsterdam's harbor. The British demanded that the Dutch surrender, but Peter Stuyvesant was prepared to fight. What a stupid man! Some of the more prominent citizens convinced him not to fight the British because he would no doubt lose.

Immediately, England seized control and reestablished a less violent relationship with the Lenape. The British were far more interested in owning land than simply trading for furs and pelts. And they even paid the Lenape for the land they inhabited, which was a totally different concept and not always easy for the Lenape to understand.

Nine years after the British took control, another Anglo-Dutch War was fought in 1773; it ended with the Dutch retaking Manhattan with six hundred soldiers. So obviously the Dutch are good at both trading and fighting.

Wait a minute! One year later, the British would take it all back again in some kind of global trade? Are you kidding me? And no Dutch were kicked out, and no property was seized. Huh? The Dutch were even permitted to have their own mayors. Their special Dutch culture would still be allowed to exist. Their architectural style continued to influence new buildings. Their naming of places was also permitted, such as Brooklyn (Breuckelen), Harlem (Haarlem), Coney Island (Conyne Eylandt) and Broadway (Breede Wegh). Hey, these English conquerors ain't so bad.

Today, the so-called Wyckoff House, built in Brooklyn about 1652 by the Dutch, still stands. Some historians even give credit to the Dutch for helping influence what was written in the Declaration of Independence and the Bill of Rights. Thank you, Dutch people!

THOSE CLEVER DUTCH

Just as we've all been amazed by what William Shakespeare (1564–1616) wrote, some of which we utilize today as common expressions of speech, the Dutch came up with some amazing phrases before Shakespeare was even born. They may surprise you, but here are a few of them:

Birds of a feather flock together.
When the cat's away, the mice will play.
To bang one's head against a brick wall.
Move like your ass is on fire!
One shears sheep, the other shears pigs. (One has all the advantages, the other has none.)
It depends on the fall of the cards. (Let the chips falls where they may.)
Two fools under one hood. (Stupidity loves company.)
To be pissing against the moon. (To be pissing into the wind.)
They both crap through the same hole. (Bosom buddies.)
If the blind lead the blind, both will fall in the ditch. (The blind leading the blind.)
It is ill to swim against the current. (An uphill battle.)
He who has spilt his porridge cannot scrape it all up again. (Don't cry over spilt milk.)
Two dogs over one bone seldom agree. (To argue uselessly over a single point).
Sitting on hot coals. (To be impatient.)
To hang one's cloak according to the wind. (To adapt one's viewpoint to the current opinion.)
The whole world is upside down.
To have the roof tiled with tarts. (To be very wealthy).
To sit between two stools in the ashes. (To be indecisive.)
To be able to tie even the devil to a pillow. (Perseverance overcomes everything.)
To crap on the world. (To despise everything.)
A pillar-biter. (A religious hypocrite.)
To lead each other by the nose. (To fool each other.)
To have the world spinning on one's thumb. (To have the world in the palm of your hand.)
To put a spoke in someone's wheel. (To throw a wrench in someone's plans.)
Horse droppings are not figs. (Appearances are deceiving.)
To try to kill two flies with one stroke. (To kill two birds with one stone.)

Very clever proverbs, but let's get back to our story.

THE BEGINNING OF THE END

One does not sell the land people walk on.

—Crazy Horse

The British purchasing land from the Indians was far more civilized than violently seizing their property. Nevertheless, it probably wasn't always a fair deal for the Lenape, especially if they received a meager amount of whatever the English offered them. And even more importantly, the Indians thought they were being paid for the use of their land, not ownership. Something in the contract got lost in translation, obviously.

In the end, the British settlers purchased a great deal of land from the Lenape. Eventually, members of the tribes started moving northward and westward to get away from the settlers. Those who stayed were subject to several restrictions regarding their movement from one location to another. And of course, the immigrants introduced the Lenape to intoxicating beverages made with alcohol. And if that wasn't bad enough to dull their senses, many succumbed to diseases such as tuberculosis, smallpox and measles.

By 1700, the local Lenape population was reduced from about two thousand tribal members to only five hundred.

In the following years, the Lenape started believing they could get their land back from the English by collaborating with the French during the French and Indian War. It didn't work out the way they had hoped. They were defeated.

By 1758, the governor of New Jersey met with the leader of the Lenape. They smoked the proverbial peace pipe and exchanged niceties. Soon after the meeting, the New Jersey Assembly established a permanent home for the Lenape in Burlington County. It was the first Indian reservation in America. In exchange, the Lenape gave up all rights to any land outside of the reservation except for the ability to hunt and fish in other areas. The reservation, however, must have seemed like a prison to the Lenape.

Other tribes, such as the Oneida, which was part of the Algonquin Nation in New York State, invited the tribe in New Jersey to become part of their village.

By 1801, the New Jersey Assembly had sold the reservation and presented the proceeds to the remaining members of the tribe, fewer than eighty-five people. About a year later, the chief of the tribe in New Jersey led his people in twelve rented wagons to New Stockbridge, New York. Some of the tribe stayed behind and moved into the local communities in southern New Jersey or the hills of northern New Jersey and Pennsylvania.

5

THE SETTLERS

EARLY SETTLERS AND IMMIGRANTS

The bosom of America is open to receive not only the opulent and respected stranger, but the oppressed and persecuted of all nations and religions; whom we shall welcome to a participation of all our rights and privileges.
—*George Washington*

Let's imagine what our ancestors first saw as their ships sailed toward America and into Raritan Bay during the early 1600s.

We've been included on a ship of Dutch traders who are making their way toward this country with the expectation of trading with whatever people they meet upon their arrival. We've been traveling for many months in the open ocean, and it's incredibly doubtful we saw another ship during our journey. And it's safe to say we really don't know exactly what we'll find when we finally arrive.

Then it becomes clear to all of us. We can make out land; it appears to be almost rising up out of the sea.

The first thing we'd probably see as our ship approaches the area is the high ground known today as Highlands on our left and the high ground on our right called Staten Island. To some, they looked like faraway islands.

A seagull may have flown over the deck to welcome us as a friendly assurance our destination was now near. Maybe we'd see land in a matter of hours, or perhaps sooner. We would all be anxious to see this new world of possibilities for trade. Maybe everyone would be rich as a result.

And then just ahead, we start seeing the white sandy beaches of Sandy Hook. The ship's bell is rung, and everyone rushes to the bow and then to the starboard side of the ship to see for themselves before quickly getting back to the important work of guiding the ship through what appeared to be an opening at the end of the spit.

We see dangerous shoals to our left (portside) and to our right (starboard). We praise God for helping to guide us this far. Tenacity, teamwork and navigational skills would be put into action before any of us could rest, however.

And then, as we pass the tip of Sandy Hook, we look to our right and see the hills of Staten Island. To our left are the hills of Highlands, which we believe is the best direction to steer our ship. As we move closer to the mouth of the Shrewsbury River, we find a place to drop anchor and secure our riggings. Once done, we assess our position and look around to view this beautiful new land. After being at sea for months and smelling nothing but the salt water, we can now sniff the scents of fresh plants, swampy marshes and fragrant flowers.

How far we had come using the crude maps made by those who came before us. How exhilarated we were when reaching our destination, and we're now ready to explore, to look for additional food supplies and water and to find the local Native Americans with whom we would begin trading.

We gather our wits and a few supplies, board a small boat and row eagerly to the shore, where the keel of our boat comes to rest in a brackish marsh. As we leave our boat and stomp through tall grasses toward fresh beaches devoid of human footsteps, we look for signs of life and the potential danger that could come without warning. As we walk along these beautiful beaches, each of us, in turn, looks toward the hills, which we will eventually climb for a better view. While the trees and plants encountered aren't entirely alien to us, it feels like we're walking on the moon.

Some two hundred years later, the so-called Poet of the American Revolution, Philip Freneau, wrote about what these early settlers and immigrants might have seen and described themselves in a poem called "Neversink":

Neversink, by Philip Freneau (1752–1832)

These Hills, the pride of all the coast,
To mighty distance seen,
With aspect bold and rugged brow,
That shade the neighboring main:
These heights, for solitude design'd,
This rude, resounding shore—
These vales impervious to the wind,
Tall oaks, that to the tempest bend,
Half Druid, I adore.
From distant lands, a thousand sails
Your hazy summits greet—
You saw the angry Briton come,
You saw him, last, retreat!
With towering crest, you first appear
The news of land to tell;
To him that comes, fresh joys impart,
To him that goes, a heavy heart,
The lover's long farewell.

'Tis your's to see the sailor bold,
Of persevering mind,
To see him rove in search of care,
And leave true bliss behind;
To see him spread his flowing sails
To trace a tiresome road,
By wintry seas and tempests chac'd
To see him o'er the ocean haste,
A comfortless abode!

Your thousand springs of waters blue
What luxury to sip,
As from the mountain's breast they flow
To moisten Flora's lip!
In vast retirements herd the deer,
Where forests round them rise,
Dark groves, their tops in æther lost,
That, haunted still by Huddy's* ghost,
The trembling rustic flies.

Proud heights! with pain so often seen,
(With joy beheld once more)
On your firm base I take my stand,
Tenacious of the shore:——
Let those who pant for wealth or fame
Pursue the watery road;——
Soft sleep and ease, blest days and nights,
And health, attend these favourite heights,
Retirement's blest abode!

*Refers to Patriot Joshua Huddy, who we'll talk about later.

Incidentally, the word *Neversink* in Freneau's poem evolved into Navesink over time. Some historians believe the name was a description of the area from sailors heading home toward Europe. As they looked back over their shoulders, they would remark that the land "never sinks" on the increasingly distant horizon. It does make sense. Long before formalized names of villages or towns, the early maps called the higher elevations simply "the high lands of neversink." Today, the so-called Highlands of Navesink stand guard over Raritan Bay and the channel, which leads to New York Harbor.

LENAPE WELCOME WAGON

I have fought for my countrymen, the squaws and papooses, against white men, who came year after year, to cheat them and take away their lands. You know the cause of our making war. It is known to all white men. They ought to be ashamed of it.

—Chief Black Hawk

As you now know, the first permanent European settlement in the region was established on Governors Island in New York Harbor in 1624, and another settlement was built eight years later in Brooklyn. Before long, these two settlements would be connected by ferry.

In 1643, two of the first immigrants, John and Penelope Kent, sailed into Raritan Bay from the Netherlands. They were excited about coming to New Amsterdam (today's New York City), but as they entered the local waters, their ship began foundering and soon made an emergency anchorage at Sandy Hook.

Unfortunately, Penelope's husband was too ill to travel any longer, so she helped him off the ship, into a small boat and onto the shore of Sandy Hook. The ship's anchor was soon pulled up, and the vessel floated away toward New York Harbor, perhaps with promises from the captain of returning with help after they reached their destination.

When the ship was gone from their sight, Lenape Indians who were on Sandy Hook at the time suddenly appeared and attacked both of them. They killed Penelope's husband before scalping her and then cutting her open to expose her intestines. The Lenape left her for dead.

Barely alive and experiencing intense pain, she crawled to a shelter in a hollow tree. Suffering much, she finally made herself known to the Lenape and prayed they would end her misery by killing her. Instead, they actually treated her wounds and cared for her. When she was well enough to travel, Penelope was released to the Dutch at New Amsterdam.

Long story short, she healed completely before meeting and marrying a man named Richard Stout a year after her attack. She was twenty-two years of age. Eventually, they had a large family (seven sons and four daughters) and lived mostly in Gravesend, which was located in present-day Coney Island in New York. Then in 1665, she and her family moved to Middletown, New Jersey, where the Lenape had originally helped her survive her wounds.

In some versions of the story, the native chief who rescued Penelope many years earlier warned her of a raid being planned by the indigenous people of the area, and she was able to prevent it from happening.

Five years after Penelope and her husband were attacked by the Lenape, the Dutch had constructed the first wharf from the island of Manhattan into the lower East River, where it would be sheltered from the elements. It was called Schreyers Hook Dock, located near today's Pearl and Broad Streets. This dock helped make the city an important port. British officials gave the leaders of New Netherland complete control over the dock and the waterfront, at least for the time being.

SHIPWRECKS

The channel is known only to the natives; so that if any stranger should enter into the bay without one of their pilots he would run great danger of shipwreck.

—*Thomas More*

The days of pure exploration were fast coming to an end. Now was the time of increasing immigration to the New World. Instead of ships coming every few decades, settlers were now coming far more frequently for a variety of reasons: to make a new life, to escape religious persecution, to make lots of money or to find adventure, in addition to any number of other reasons.

The shipping traffic in Raritan Bay and back to Europe was becoming an issue, however, because shipwrecks were regularly occurring due to many dangerous conditions. Today, there are at least six thousand documented shipwrecks along the coast of New Jersey, and the entrance to Raritan Bay was becoming known as a significant challenge to any ships approaching it.

The entire geography of Sandy Hook has been victimized by the ravaging tides, wave action, storms and wind, which have caused the beaches, as well as Sandy Hook itself, to continually physically change. During the winter, the beaches are steeper, and by early spring, the sand of the beach sand consists of more quartz gravel. The relentless wind during the winter creates sand rich in garnet, magnetite, hematite and other minerals. During the summer, the gravel and minerals diminish or even disappear. As a result of the changing shape of Sandy Hook and shifting sands of shoals beneath the surrounding water, the ships that tried to enter Raritan Bay often met tragic ends.

The *Castle Del Key* was one such ship, with 132 people killed of the 145 crew members on board. While the records from 1705 are a bit sketchy, the boat most likely was a privateer vessel with eighteen guns. Privateers were like government-sanctioned pirates who would plunder other ships on behalf of either a government or investors. The profits from the plundering would be split. The *Castle Del Key* was wrecked on a shoal near Sandy Hook after fighting against gale-force winds during a cold winter storm.

Some ships never made it to the entrance of our harbor, such as the *New Era*, which was on its maiden voyage bringing German immigrants to New York. It ran aground in 1854 near today's Asbury Park with some 220 to 284 lives lost.

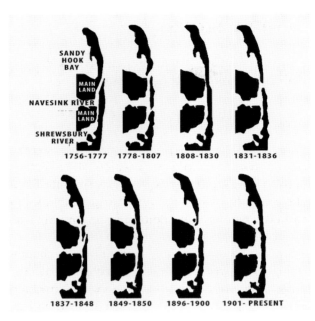

Left: Changing shape of Sandy Hook, New Jersey.

Below: The *Morrow Castle*.

At the time, witnesses described people in chaos attempting to escape the ship as it began sinking. Most of them couldn't speak English. People on the shore were unable to help and simply watched the tragedy. Some of the immigrants tried to swim ashore but were unable to reach it.

Today, the anchor from the *New Era*, which was retrieved in 1999, is located at the Church of St. Andrew's by-the-Sea in Allenhurst, New Jersey.

Also lost during the same year as the *Castle Del Key* was the *Powhattan*, which was transporting mail from England. It was also carrying German immigrants to New York. Reports indicate some 311 to 365 lives were lost after the ship ran aground near Long Beach Island at the Barnegat Shoals. The following day, the ship sank. The victims began turning up on beaches along the coast as far down as Atlantic City. They were buried in local cemeteries, such as Smithville Methodist Church, where a memorial exists to remember the victims.

The *Morro Castle* was a well-known shipwreck because so many people witnessed it. The 508-foot ocean liner was heading for New York when it caught fire in 1934 near Long Beach Island before coming to a stop on the beach at Asbury Park. Crowds of people watched it burn as the surf broke against its hull.

SAVING LIVES AT SEA

If the ship is sinking, you need help getting off that ship.
—*Richard Quest*

These were just a few of the thousands of shipwrecks that occurred over the centuries in our area. But it wasn't only ships and cargo that were threatened; it was lives. Therefore, small lifesaving stations were built beginning in 1849 on America's East Coast, where ships would frequently get wrecked. At first, the stations were run by volunteers. By 1878, Congress had established the U.S. Life-Saving Service and began paying six-member crews who would tend each of the forty stations located in New Jersey.

There were two lifesaving stations on Sandy Hook. One was located near the tip of the Hook, while the other was near Spermaceti Cove. Both stations looked like typical backyard sheds, except there were no lawnmowers. Instead, the sheds were filled with rescue equipment. Today, you can visit one of the actual sheds at the Twin Lights of Navesink in Highlands, New Jersey.

Lifesaving station, circa 1898. *Courtesy of the National Park Service.*

Wreck of *Edmund J. Phinney* off Sandy Hook.

Each station's rescue equipment included a surfboat mounted on a wagon, a small line-throwing mortar and a small enclosed metal lifeboat called a life-car that could contain up to six passengers.

The rescue team would fire a claw-like hook and rope line toward a ship in distress. After the ship's crew fastened the hook directly to the vessel, the rescue team would send the life-car via the rope to the ship. Endangered passengers would enter the life-car six people at a time. After the life-car was sealed to become watertight, the rescue crew would pull the rope attached to the life-car from the shore to haul them back to the beach. Rescue teams, composed of what were called surfmen, would practice this technique daily. The work was both physically demanding and dangerous.

For example, in 1907, the *Edmund J. Phinney* was wrecked during a storm almost one thousand feet from the beaches of Sandy Hook. The rescue crew pulled their equipment more than two miles over flooded beaches against a powerful wind to save a crew of ten. They were successful.

From 1871 through 1914, the U.S. Life-Saving Service tried to rescue some 28,000 ships and rescued more than 178,000 people, while 1,455 people lost their lives.

As iron-hulled steamships replaced sailing ships, the role of the lifesaving service was changing. In 1915, the U.S. Life-Saving Service merged with another agency to form the U.S. Coast Guard, which continues its presence at the tip of Sandy Hook and maintains the light in the Sandy Hook Lighthouse.

6

THE LIGHTHOUSES

LIGHTING THE WAY

I can think of no other edifice constructed by man as altruistic as a lighthouse. They were built only to serve.

—*George Bernard Shaw*

Saving lives was always extremely important work, but the businesses and investors who lost ships wanted some assurance their profits would not sink with their vessels. They were entrepreneurs, companies and traders trying to move their goods back and forth, quickly and efficiently.

Not everyone had a smooth crossing, and many of the goods being transported for profit or trade were being lost at sea either because of storms, poor navigation or pirates and privateers. The people who funded many of these voyages were not at all happy about losing their cargo.

Colonists and businesses also feared an attack from the French, so they lit kegs of oil at night and large flammable balls during the day, which could be raised when enemy ships were spotted coming into the harbor. Observers would then alert New York City when the beacons were activated. Unfortunately, one of the beacons was accidentally lit in 1746, but no alarm was sounded in the city. This failure was enough to eliminate any confidence in the warning system and resulted in a firm reprimand of those in New York who failed to report what they should have seen.

The main concern of businesses was finding a way for ships to know how to navigate into Raritan Bay and New York Harbor safely without being shipwrecked. Therefore, beginning in 1740, a primitive light beacon was established in the hills of Highlands near the site of today's lighthouse called the Twin Lights of Navesink.

While the first set of twin lights was undoubtedly helpful, the lights were not entirely sufficient for the ships that ran aground because they didn't see the tip of Sandy Hook until it was too late. Therefore, the Sandy Hook Lighthouse—located on the grounds of the now historic and decommissioned Fort Hancock—was built in 1764. Today, it's the oldest working lighthouse in the United States, but lighthouses, in general, are becoming defunct, as more and more technological advancements are being made to aid in marine navigation.

Interestingly, when the lighthouse was first built, it was located only five hundred feet from the tip of Sandy Hook, but Mother Nature and continual tidal changes have added more land around the base. As a result, the lighthouse is about one and a half miles farther from the tip of Sandy Hook.

Incidentally, with the start of the American Revolution (explained later in our story), the lighthouse was deliberately disabled before the arrival of the British fleet. Orders were given to remove the lighting apparatus and oil from the lighthouse so that if it fell into the enemy's hands, it would be useless. Unfortunately, within several months of the British occupying Sandy Hook, the lighthouse was repaired and re-enabled.

Undeterred, the American forces led an attack to destroy the lighthouse so it could not be used by the British to help their ships navigate back and forth during the war. American cannons fired on the lighthouse for more than an hour. No damage could be done, however. When the British increased their efforts to protect the lighthouse, the Americans retreated. Sadly, the British would retain control of the lighthouse for most of the war.

On the western edge of Sandy Hook, which faces Highlands, the spit (as it's technically called) is affected by tidal currents and waves generated by wind across Raritan Bay. As a result, there are several tidal and current-constructed sandbars and small islands on the bayside near the mouths of the Navesink Estuary and Shrewsbury River. For example, Plum Island is a remnant of an old tidal inlet formed by several intense storms that separated Sandy Hook from the mainland during the 1800s. Also, the west side of the peninsula contains a few tidal creeks that drain the salt marshes. Historically, the central portion of Sandy Hook includes a substrate of an ancient beach that has been buried.

So despite continual changes in the landscape of Sandy Hook and shifting shoals (or sandbars) near whatever channel existed, the lighthouse was helpful to captains entering the southern end of New York Harbor. The lighthouse was initially called New York Lighthouse because it was funded through a New York Assembly lottery as well as with a tax on all ships entering the Port of New York.

By now, it must come as no surprise that Sandy Hook was a strategically important piece of property for defending our country and for guiding ships with supplies and immigrants into Raritan Bay and eventually into New York Harbor.

Less than fifty years after the Sandy Hook Lighthouse was built in 1746, an additional pair of beacons were constructed in the hills of Highlands.

Almost twenty years after their construction, the two mostly wooden towers in Highlands were beginning to show signs of wear and tear. In 1862, they were replaced with a castle-like brownstone structure with an octagonal tower on the north side and a square tower located 228 feet away on the opposite end. Also, a two-story residence for the lighthouse keeper and his assistant was to be located between the two towers. Additional living quarters for other assistants were located within the wings, which attached the towers to the two-story dwelling.

The Twin Lights of Navesink in Highlands, New Jersey.

Incidentally, a historic event occurred at the Twin Lights of Navesink in 1893: the public reading of America's national oath of loyalty for the first time. Known today as the Pledge of Allegiance, it was first read at an outdoor ceremony next to a 135-foot-high flagpole (Liberty Pole). The first official recitation was led by its author, Francis Bellamy, who wrote the Pledge of Allegiance for schoolchildren to recite during a Columbus Day ceremony in 1892.

Meanwhile, at the World's Columbian Exposition of 1893, a new and innovative Fresnel lens was displayed by the French. Rather than transport the seven-ton lens back to France after the exposition, the French convinced the United States to purchase it for the Twin Lights of Navesink.

Unfortunately, the lens required electricity, so a temporary structure was built behind the south tower to run an electrical generator. By 1898, the lens and arc lamp produced twenty-five million candlepower. This effectively made the Twin Lights of Navesink the first coastal light to use electricity, which also made it the most powerful beacon in America.

The revolving lens produced a flash of light every five seconds that could be seen for more than twenty-two miles out at sea. The permanent brick powerhouse seen today was built in 1910.

Unfortunately, folks living in the communities of Highlands and Navesink complained about not being able to sleep because the light was too bright. They complained about their chickens not laying eggs, and their cows were refusing to provide them with milk. As a result, three panels in the south tower were placed in the direction of the complaining town folk. Even the lighthouse keepers had to wear special goggles when they worked near the light to protect their eyes.

In 1899, another historic event was Guglielmo Marconi's public demonstration of the first wireless telegraph for sending and receiving messages regularly. After installing a high antenna next to the twin lights as well as the necessary equipment, he was able to receive reports from a ship in the ocean on the progress of a naval review honoring the return of Commodore George Dewey from the Spanish-American War's Battle of Manila Bay.

For the next fifty years, different lenses and lights were used at the Twin Lights as technology advanced. Finally, the Twin Lights of Navesink shut down in 1949. The Borough of Highlands, located just below the lights, was given ownership of the Twin Lights in 1954 but gave it to the State of New Jersey in 1962 because the town was unable to maintain it properly. Today, the Twin Lights of Navesink is listed in the State and National Registers of Historic Places.

Guglielmo Marconi.

So, with two critically essential lighthouses in Highlands and on Sandy Hook, shipwrecks were not as frequent. While the ships coming into Raritan Bay and New York Harbor were feeling a bit safer, the local fishing boats were still worried, mostly at the western end of Raritan Bay.

In the 1800s, the fishing and farming industries were quite lucrative and helped support a fast-growing population now living around the bay and in the farmlands beyond. Harvesting oysters and clams was hard but lucrative work.

Unfortunately, because there were so many boats in Raritan Bay and oysters were becoming so plentiful just off the southern end of Staten Island, where the water from the Raritan River and Arthur Kill merged, there were shipwrecks on a great bed of oysters.

The oysters had multiplied greatly, probably because the State of New Jersey had passed a law in 1719 that stated oysters could not be gathered in order to conserve them. Only the Lenape—what few of them remained in the area—could harvest the oysters.

In 1878, the federal government finally responded to a petition by local ship owners and businesspeople for the construction of a lighthouse on the most enormous oyster bed in Raritan Bay to signal ships of the danger below the surface of the water. Eventually, the plethora of oysters would completely disappear by the 1940s as a result of pollution. More about their demise later.

Great Beds Lighthouse.

In 1880, however, the Great Beds Lighthouse was erected directly over the mound of oysters at the bottom of Raritan Bay. The tower comprised five iron sections rising forty-two feet high out of the water. It utilized a Fresnel lens within the decagonal lantern room to cast its beams of red light out over Raritan Bay with a focal plane of fifty-seven feet.

The first keeper of the Great Beds Lighthouse served for just under two years before resigning. His replacement lived on the tiny island inside the lighthouse and rarely visited the shore except to obtain provisions or to receive his pay. One day he visited Perth Amboy to receive his salary. In the evening, he started rowing back to the lighthouse as the weather grew worse. He had noticed that the light wasn't burning for some reason.

Several people had tried to dissuade him from trying to reach the lighthouse in the stormy weather, but he laughed at the idea that he wouldn't be able to manage his boat and insisted that the light had to be lit that night. One woman was so concerned for the keeper that she sat at her window and watched as his boat was tossed as he moved across the water, and after a severe struggle, he finally came closer to the lighthouse.

Just as he was preparing to disembark, the boat quickly moved away from the lighthouse. The next morning, his boat washed ashore. His body was found three weeks after he disappeared. Only $40 of the roughly $150 he was thought to be carrying was found on his body.

The next keeper of the lighthouse had an even shorter career as the lightkeeper during 1883. He, too, mysteriously disappeared. His boat was found tied to the lighthouse with his coat inside. His keys were on the table inside the lighthouse. Some believed that he killed himself by jumping into Raritan Bay, while others think he disappeared for some other nefarious purpose.

Eventually, the Great Beds Lighthouse was deactivated in 2011 and sold at auction for $90,000 to a retired contractor who died two years after his purchase. Perhaps the lighthouse is cursed.

Another lighthouse floated. It was called *Lightship Ambrose*, and several lightships were so named from 1823 until 1967. The original was only the fourth lightship designed and commissioned to serve a port on the coast of the United States. The first *Lightship Ambrose* is now a moored museum in New York City. We can see it from our small boat between the southern tip of Manhattan and the Brooklyn Bridge.

There were many other lighthouses scattered throughout Raritan Bay in the early days before electronic and GPS-guided navigation.

Lightship *Ambrose*.

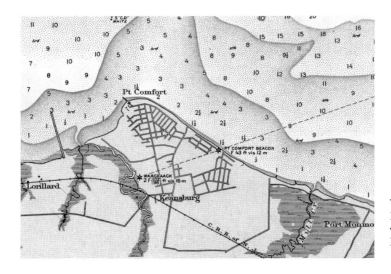

Waackaack Light aligning with a light on Raritan Bay, 1924.

Three of them were positioned along the approach to New York Harbor during the 1850s: Chapel Hill Rear Range Light on Sandy Hook Bay, New Dorp Light in the namesake section of Staten Island and the Point Comfort Light (aka Bayside Beacon) in Keansburg, New Jersey—all nearly identical lighthouses.

Incidentally, the New Dorp Lighthouse was decommissioned and boarded up in 1964. The lighthouse and land were neglected and subsequently vandalized until sold at auction to a resident of Staten Island who restored the lighthouse to become his private residence. As a result, it is not open to the public. New Dorp Light was designated a New York City Landmark in 1967 and listed in the National Register of Historic Places in 1973.

While some of the old lighthouses are still standing and can be visited by the public, there are others long gone from view. The two lighthouses in Keansburg, New Jersey, operated in conjunction with each other, much like the Twin Lights of Navesink, but are now gone.

The first light was called Bayside Beacon, and it sat on the shore of Raritan Bay. The second, higher light was called Waackaack Light; it stood 102 feet tall and was located three quarters of a mile farther inland on Creek Road.

If you drew a straight line from light to light and then extended it in an easterly direction, it would line up directly with the shipping channel next to the tip of Sandy Hook. Therefore, ships in the harbor would set their course by lining up both lights to determine their position in the bay.

The second light in Keansburg was Bayside Beacon, which was built in 1856. The original wooden structure served as the lightkeeper's home and was replaced by a forty-five-foot metal tower in 1919. The Bayside Beacon tower still exists in Leonardo, New Jersey. The tower had been taken by the U.S. Army Corps of Engineers in 1941 to replace the aging octagonal tower on the lower range in Leonardo. The appropriated tower is now known as Conover Lighthouse.

On the northern side of Raritan Bay is Prince's Bay Light, which is officially called John Cardinal O'Connor Light. Constructed in 1864 for the sum of $30,000, it is located on the highest point of the southern shoreline on an eighty-five-foot bluff with an attached brownstone cottage that served as the lightkeeper's house. As stated before, the bluffs are part of the southern terminal moraine formed by the Wisconsin Glacier, which started receding some ten thousand years ago.

The Prince's Bay Lighthouse was deactivated in 1922. The lighthouse, the bluffs and 145 acres of surrounding upland and 49 underwater acres were purchased in 1999 from the Archdiocese of New York by New York State and the Trust for Public Land.

Across the Narrows of New York Harbor in Raritan Bay, just off the coastline of Staten Island, is Old Orchard Light, which stands thirty-five feet tall. Placed into service in 1893, it can be seen about three miles from the Crooke's Point area in Great Kills State Park.

Old Orchard Light.

Romer Shoal Light, 1916. *Courtesy of Jeremy D'Entremont.*

Romer Shoal Light is an iconic National Landmark lighthouse in Lower New York Harbor, on the north edge of the Swash Channel, south of Ambrose Channel and north of Sandy Hook at the entrance to New York Harbor. After its brief role as a land-based training light at the National Lighthouse Keepers Academy on Staten Island, it was moved to its current location in 1898. The light was added to the National Register of Historic Places in 2007 as Romer Shoal Light Station. Romer Shoal marks a dangerous shoal east of New York Harbor's Ambrose Channel with a light and foghorn.

West Bank Light, officially West Bank Front Range Light, is in Lower New York Bay and acts as the front range light for the Ambrose Channel. It is currently active and not open to the public. The tower was built in 1901 and heightened in 1908.

Fort Wadsworth Light is a 1903 lighthouse built atop Battery Weed on Staten Island in New York Harbor. The light illuminates the Narrows, which is the main entrance to New York Harbor. Located under the Verrazano-Narrows Bridge, Fort Wadsworth Light was part of the transfer of Fort Wadsworth from the U.S. Navy to the National Park Service in 1995 as part of Gateway National Recreation Area. Its light was visible for fourteen nautical miles. When the Verrazano-Narrows Bridge opened in 1965, the lighthouse became obsolete. Dark for many years, it was restored and converted to solar power by volunteers in 2005.

The Staten Island Range Light, also known as the Ambrose Channel Range Light, is the rear range light companion to the West Bank Lighthouse. Built in 1912, the 90-foot tower sits more than five miles northwest of the West Bank Lighthouse on Staten Island's Richmond Hill (Lighthouse Hill), 141 feet above sea level. It was designated a New York City Landmark in 1968 and remained a valuable aid to navigation for those ships entering the Ambrose Channel in Lower New York Bay. It was listed in the National Register of Historic Places in 2005.

West Bank Light.

Ambrose Light, often called Ambrose Tower, was the light station at the convergence of several major shipping lanes in Lower New York Bay, including Ambrose Channel, the primary passage for ships entering and departing the Port of New York and New Jersey. In 2008, the Coast Guard announced that Ambrose Light, which was severely damaged when a tanker struck it in 2007, would be dismantled. The Coast Guard has replaced the light with flashing buoys.

Light Station Ambrose was put into operation in 1967, replacing the obsolete *Lightship Ambrose*. The tower design was like the famous Texas

Fort Wadsworth Light. *Courtesy of Steven L. Markos.*

Tower, a strong steel-pipe structure based on the oil platforms built for use in the Gulf of Mexico. The tower station was situated about seven miles from Sandy Hook in about 70 feet of water. The tower was supported by four 42-inch diameter steel pipes, which were sunk down 245 feet to the bedrock below.

The light was about 136 feet above mean low-water level and the 10 million candlepower light could be seen for 18 miles. The lower deck was designed for fuel and water storage while the top deck served as living quarters for a crew of fewer than ten. The roof of the platform also served as a flight deck for helicopters, which was the primary mode of transportation for crew members going to and from the station.

Eventually, the tower was automated in 1988, so the crew was no longer required. On a clear night in 1996, however, a 754-foot Greek oil tanker called *Aegeo* struck the tower and caused severe damage. *Aegeo*'s captain was found to be at fault. By 1999, the entire tower had been dismantled as a result of damages from the accident.

A new tower was built less than two miles east of the old site, but as luck would have it, a 492-foot Maltese freighter struck the new tower. The light

Staten Island Range Light. *Courtesy of Jim Henderson.*

was rendered inoperable, so a temporary lighted buoy was set afloat by the U.S. Coast Guard.

Today, as navigational technology advances, reliance on the traditional system of lighthouses has diminished. However, there are probably ship captains who still use compasses and rely on lighthouses and beacons to guide them back to port, around dangerous shoals or past other submerged obstacles. With the vast amounts of technology available today, such as GPS and radar, there's plenty of equipment available, particularly if you are a large commercial vessel.

Unfortunately, you and I are in my small boat. We don't have even a tenth of the gadgets available to assist us in effortless navigation. But right now, we have more to worry about than merely navigating this boat from Point A to Point B. We have to start worrying about pirates!

7

THE PIRATES

PIRATES AND PRIVATEERS

You can always trust the untrustworthy because you can always trust that they will be untrustworthy. It's the trustworthy you can't trust.
—*Captain Jack Sparrow in the movie* Pirates of the Caribbean

So let's go back to the late seventeenth and early eighteenth centuries when ships with both cargo and passengers were entering Raritan Bay and then New York Harbor in droves. And we're floating in our boat among them.

The merchant ships were bringing supplies to the New World to help fuel the building of a new country. Then they'd return to their home countries with whatever goods they were able to find to make the trip worthwhile. Unfortunately, Sandy Hook and Raritan Bays were filled with pirates who would attack these merchant ships.

The infamous Blackbeard conducted raids into Middletown, and Captain Morgan also came to our area frequently to intimidate the local settlers. These pirates were a bit like the Mafia in those days. If you were a business or shipowner, you would pay the pirates a so-called protection fee, and they'd leave you alone. In fact, many local colonial families made their fortunes by either investing in the expedition of pirates or buying stolen goods from them and reselling the stolen treasures to their customers.

Blackbeard, the pirate.

Captain Kidd. *National Maritime Historical Society.*

Strangely, professional pirating was encouraged in this area because a number of the residents were profiting from their exploits.

One of the most colorful pirates of the day was Captain Kidd, who eventually turned from pirating to government-sanctioned privateering. Kidd was granted a license by the king of England that authorized him to seize and capture French and pirate ships. He agreed to split what he was able to steal or plunder with England as well as any financial backers who had invested in his operation.

In 1696, Kidd left England for New York City. Unfortunately, on his way to America, a British warship pulled alongside of Kidd's ship to draft much of his crew into service for the Royal Navy. The apprehension of his crew forced him to recruit new crewmembers when he reached America. He would also have to pay the new crew a larger share of the booty, or profit. And for a while, he would act on orders from England to attack certain vessels or locations in other countries. After a number of these missions, Kidd began to stray from the direct orders of his king and returned to piracy so he would not have to share the profits with anyone.

He would occasionally drop anchor in Raritan Bay and row to shore to bury his treasure in strategic locations in Monmouth County, New Jersey. He claimed to have £40,000 hidden in a chest somewhere along Raritan Bay, but rumors said it was more like £400,000.

Interestingly, according to historical records, Captain Kidd provided the rope and tackle from his ship to help hoist the stones used in building the first Trinity Church on Wall Street in New York City in 1698. See? He was one of the good pirates.

Eventually, Kidd was captured and returned to England to face trial for his many crimes. He was found guilty of murder and piracy and then sentenced to be hanged in 1701. After his death, Kidd's body was covered with tar, bound in chains and hung from a bridge on the Thames River in London to warn other pirates. His body remained hanging there on the bridge until it decayed some years later.

After his death, some £20,000 in treasure was discovered on Gardiner's Island off the coast of Long Island, New York. Kidd had left his treasure with Jonathon Gardiner, who cooperated with British authorities in retrieving it. But there were other locations rumored to have treasure buried, such as Cape May, where pirates visited to obtain fresh water. Another place to search for treasure may well have been in Toms River, where pirates could easily hide. But yet another location could have been Sandy Hook because Kidd anchored there for a while during his final visit to Raritan Bay.

Many years ago, someone found Spanish gold coins from the seventeenth century on Money Island in Raritan Bay just off the shoreline of today's Cliffwood Beach. Unfortunately, the island no longer exists. Adding to the intrigue, however, someone also found gold coins in a small lake called Duck Pond, now known as Treasure Lake.

And here's one more thing that may help you in your search for treasure. At one time, there were two large elm trees known as Kidd's Rangers. One was located at the mouth of Matawan Creek in Keyport, and the other was located at Fox Hill in today's Rose Hill Cemetery. According to the legend, these trees were the markers Kidd used to guide him back to his treasure.

Today, people still search for treasure at Cliffwood Beach and find bits of gold and silver, but nobody has found the mother lode. Not yet. In 1948, however, a seventy-five-year-old lobsterman found several gold coins (dated 1730 and later) on a beach in Highlands, New Jersey, directly across from Sandy Hook. When he showed his friends the coins, word spread like wildfire. Within hours, the beach where he found the coins was filled with treasure hunters.

Even local businesses closed as thousands of people invaded Highlands to look for what they thought was part of Captain Kidd's treasure. Unfortunately, these coins couldn't have been part of Kidd's treasure because he was hanged as a pirate some thirty years before the dates on the found coins. While a few additional coins were found, no spectacular cache of gold was ever located.

8

THE BRITISH

ENGLAND'S DESIRE

I think I can save the British Empire from anything—except the British.
—Winston Churchill

It was now becoming quite obvious the British had their eye on the prize—the New World.

The British Empire comprised the territories ruled or administered by the United Kingdom and its predecessor states. It originated with the overseas possessions and trading posts established by England between the late sixteenth and early eighteenth centuries. At its height, it was the largest empire in history and, for over a century, was the foremost global power. Ah, the glory days!

Britain, however, was not alone in its thirst for power. During the fifteenth and sixteenth centuries, Portugal and Spain were first to express interest in exploring the world and establishing an empire. The empires created were capable of generating a lot of wealth, so England, France and the Netherlands started establishing colonies and trade networks of their own in the Americas and Asia.

By 1664, the British had made our area one of their many colonies throughout the world. As a result, the Dutch were squeezed out and lost New Netherlands, which we already discussed. A moment of silence, please, for the Dutch. The British then divided up New Jersey and gave control of East Jersey to Sir George Carteret and West Jersey to Lord John Berkeley. The land was officially named New Jersey after the Isle of Jersey in the English Channel.

Berkeley and Carteret sold property in their individual parts of the region to settlers looking for political and religious freedom. Before long, America became more ethnically diverse than many of the other colonies. By this time, the population of the New Jersey colony was about 100,000 people. Wow! I remember when the entire country's immigrant population was 300.

Many of the early settlers had no problems with Great Britain's role in the establishment of the original colonies of America. After all, the British helped us greatly during the French and Indian War. We didn't think we'd really need an army, a navy or even weapons to defend ourselves. We didn't even have much manufacturing capability, so many of our products were imported from the Mother Country.

Great Britain had eight million residents in 1775, while the thirteen colonies had about two and a half million people, including roughly half a million slaves. Englishman Richard Hartshorne was one of the first British settlers and purchased a large tract of land in New Jersey from the Lenape. The area soon became known as Portland Poynt and mostly included today's Atlantic Highlands, Highlands and Sandy Hook. The next village in New Jersey to be inhabited by the English settlers was called Shrewsbury, and the third was named Middletown, generally located between the two other villages.

Meanwhile, the British government was paying a large sum of money for raising, supplying and funding its army on foreign soil to defend the colonies from any attack by other countries. It was not easy being the British Empire. It was downright difficult. So many people, so many problems. But as long as the money kept flowing back to the royal coffers, everything will be just fine.

Because Americans weren't really sharing the burden of financial support, Great Britain began to levy taxes as a way to minimize the substantial cost of supporting our young country. Seems fair enough, right? Many of the colonists agreed because it made sense to them as well. You couldn't expect to live in a new world without the necessary resources for an infrastructure to support the progress of a burgeoning civilization. So, it made sense to pay a tax or two to help defray the costs.

Unfortunately, some of the British tax legislation was unpopular with colonists. Colonists began to believe it was unfair and that they, as Americans, should have elected representatives instead of being dominated by England's complete control over a fledgling society. Give us a break!

As a result, the colonists grew more and more discordant in their disputes with Jolly Old England. In reaction, the British soldiers in America began to deal with the beginnings of an American uprising with some degree of force and disrespect for the personal privacy and social interaction of Americans. It was a tense time in America, as both sides attempted to find a solution.

Americans formed Committees of Correspondence and, later, a Continental Congress, to find common ground with Great Britain, but none was found. And so it began.

VIVA REVOLUTION!

The boisterous sea of liberty is never without a wave.
—*Thomas Jefferson*

About seven hundred British troops were on a mission in Lexington, Massachusetts, to capture Patriot leaders and seize a Patriot arsenal. Captain John Parker, along with seventy-seven armed minutemen, was waiting on the town's common green. British major John Pitcairn ordered the outnumbered Patriots to disperse, and after a moment's hesitation, the Americans began to drift off the green. Suddenly, a shot was fired from an undetermined gun, and a cloud of musket smoke rose into the air. When the brief skirmish ended, eight Americans were dead or soon would be. Another ten were wounded. Only one British soldier was injured, but this was all serious enough to get us really angry. And you don't want to see us mad, because we'll revolt. The American Revolution had begun. It was April 19, 1775.

When those first shots were fired, American revolutionaries knew in their hearts that independence was the only way to end the mostly social conflict. A young America was trying at least to stand toe-to-toe with Great Britain. It was a controversial decision made by the so-called upstart American colonists. Not everyone agreed with the idea of seeking independence from the Mother Country.

There were reasonably good arguments on both sides. So, just like in today's world politics, there were some colonists who supported the notion of pushing back against Great Britain—the Patriots. And some citizens felt going to war was a mistake and that they would oppose it—the Loyalists. And then there was also a group that didn't care one way or the other. They were content to go whichever way the wind blew.

The Patriots were also known as revolutionaries, colonials, continentals, rebels, Yankees or Whigs. The Loyalists, who remained faithful to the king of Great Britain, were also known as Royalists, King's Men or Tories.

Eventually, about 231,000 men would serve in the Continental army, though never more than 48,000 at any one time and never more than 13,000 at any one place. The total number of the colonial militias numbered upward of 145,000 men. In 1799, France sent more than 12,000 soldiers to help us fight the war.

The British army had some 50,000, with an additional 25,000 Loyalists who were faithful to Great Britain. Also, some 30,000 German auxiliaries, or Hessians, were hired to fight with the British army.

An estimated 6,800 Americans were killed, while 6,100 were wounded and some 20,000 taken prisoner. An additional 17,000 people died from disease. More than 50 percent of those who died of disease did so while they were prisoners of war.

Everyone knows, of course, one of the most important documents in our history is the Declaration of Independence, which was signed on July 4, 1776. It announced to the world that America was formally ending its relationship with England.

Perth Amboy served as the colonial capital of Jersey from 1686 until 1776. During the colonial era and for a while after that, Perth Amboy was an essential waystation for traveling between Philadelphia and New York City. The slip was later used to transport newly arrived immigrants from Ellis Island, many of whom remained in the town.

TRYING TO SMOKE THE PEACE PIPE

There's a little-known vestige of our search for peace before the war got out of hand and too much bloodshed was spilled. It was a fairly secret meeting at a place called the Conference House, located at the most southern end of Staten Island. Even though it was built in about 1680, it still stands today and may be seen from our boat at the mouth of the Arthur Kill across from Perth Amboy on the southwestern tip of Staten Island (known today as Tottenville) on the former estate of Loyalist Christopher Billop.

On September 11, 1776, Continental Congress representatives John Adams, Edward Rutledge and Benjamin Franklin met with the king's representative, Lord Richard Howe, at this house on Staten Island. The

The Conference House on Staten Island, New York.

British would not consider independence a negotiable term, and the congressional representatives had been authorized only to negotiate terms that included independence. Unfortunately, both sides went back to their leaders to report a failed reconciliation. But at least we tried.

A FAMILY AFFAIR

We must all hang together, or assuredly we shall all hang separately.
—*Benjamin Franklin*

William Franklin, illegitimate son of Ben Franklin, was born about 1730. His mother's identity was unknown, but Benjamin and his common-law wife, Deborah Read, raised William as their son. William was close with his father while growing up, and as a young man, he participated in his father's famous electrical kite-flying experiment in 1752. Eventually, thirty-three-year-old William Franklin served as the royal governor of New Jersey. At that time, New Jersey was a royal colony with a governor appointed by the king of England.

There were two capitals of New Jersey then: Perth Amboy in the east and Burlington in the west. During his first eleven years as governor, William lived

Patriot Ben Franklin and Loyalist William Franklin (father and son).

in an estate in Burlington. Then in 1774, he moved to Perth Amboy to live at Proprietary House.

During William's years as royal governor of New Jersey, the tensions that would lead to the Revolutionary War began to grow throughout all of the colonies. As previously mentioned, feelings were mixed. Some people liked the idea of being an independent nation, while others enjoyed the existing relationship with Britain. This general disagreement would sometimes cause rifts within families, as it would within the Franklin family.

Shortly after the Revolutionary War began in 1775, Benjamin Franklin and his son, William, met to discuss their positions regarding independence. Neither man could convince the other of his position on the matter. Benjamin was committed to the American cause of gaining independence; William was committed to being the royal governor and remaining loyal to Britain.

The two met again briefly later in the year, and it would be their last meeting until the end of the war. During the war, each of the men remained faithful to his belief. And soon, as the war grew more intense, they would be split apart.

YOU DID WHAT?

During the Revolutionary War, the Arthur Kill—which connected western Raritan Bay with New York Harbor—served as a line of demarcation between the British who held Staten Island and the Americans who mostly controlled New Jersey.

There was a battle on Staten Island in 1777, a failed attempt by the Continental army to attack British forces. After most of the British troops had sailed from New York City, the Americans believed Staten Island was vulnerable, and they attacked. George Washington, however, wanted to reinforce the main army with troops as soon as possible to support an assault on British-held Philadelphia.

The American troops, along the shore of Arthur Kill, ignored Washington's request and charged blindly into battle by crossing Arthur Kill and entering Staten Island. The army ended up with a hodgepodge of crossed signals. As a result, the Continental troops experienced a large number of losses of dead, wounded or captured. As a result, George Washington lost the three hundred or so men he was counting on for an upcoming military campaign.

Staten Island, New York.

The commander of the raid was accused of mismanaging it. A court-martial later exonerated him of all charges.

WASHINGTON PROVES HIMSELF

Not everyone realizes how much of a significant role New Jersey played during the Revolutionary War. George Washington spent more time in New Jersey than in any other colony during the war. There must have been a lot of sleepovers for George.

New Jersey's geographic position during the war also made it a strategic location and earned it the moniker, the "Crossroads of the American Revolution." The proof of New Jersey's claim to fame was the Battle of Monmouth Courthouse, which was fought in 1778. Most historians consider the battle to be a draw. Neither side conclusively won the battle. But at the same time, it was a dramatic turning point for General Washington, who proved to the world his men could stand up against the best army in the world, the redcoats.

Before the Battle of Monmouth, the British army had chased Washington's Continental army across New Jersey and into Pennsylvania during December 1776. Washington waited until Christmas, when most of the British military believed they would be safe during the holiday. But that's when Washington made his famous crossing to New Jersey on the Delaware River and surprised the British, who immediately retreated. It was a strategic move which allowed the Continental Army to return to New Jersey.

The following month, in January, there was a clash between British and American armies near Freehold, where a much larger battle—the Battle of Monmouth Courthouse—would be fought in 1782. But this earlier smaller skirmish involved only a few hundred men, and it was over in less than fifteen minutes. While this small scrap didn't get included in the list of the most significant battles of the war, it did manage to create a cadre of committed Loyalists who would torment Patriots in the region for the next five years.

Some twenty miles south of Raritan Bay, one of the most critical battles of the war was going to provide General Washington with an opportunity to show the country his mettle.

London sent orders to the British army to leave Philadelphia and go to New York City. While both cities were equally crucial for England to

Washington Rallying the Troops at Monmouth. Emanuel Leutze.

hold, there weren't enough soldiers available to hold both for any length of time. Meanwhile, American spies in the City of Brotherly Love advised Washington of the British plans.

New York City was far more strategic to the British because it had a harbor where they could be resupplied. They were also concerned about the French naval force, which could blockade their efforts by positioning their ships at the mouth of the Delaware River.

Unfortunately, if the British let Philadelphia fall into the hands of the American forces, the Tory Loyalists located there would be vulnerable to revenge from the Patriots. Regardless, the British troops began leaving Philadelphia very early in the morning. On the New Jersey side of the Delaware River, some thousand or so rebel militia, who knew of the evacuation, were waiting for them.

Many Monday-morning quarterbacks criticized dear George Washington for not attacking the British while they spent seven hours crossing the Delaware River to reach the shores of New Jersey. In his wisdom, Washington thought his army was quite ready for a surprise attack.

It's important to note something about one of the major heroes of the Revolutionary War, Prussian baron Friedrich Wilhelm von Steuben, who helped train the new-and-improved American fighting forces while they camped at Valley Forge during a frigid and miserable winter. Von Steuben, who most people probably have never read or heard about, spoke very little English, but miraculously he did manage to teach Washington's men how to fight.

Oh, by the way, it was sweltering during the marches both armies were making to eventually meet their mutual destinies in a farm field near Freehold, New Jersey. The temperature rose to ninety degrees during the day. Severe thunderstorms occurred during the evening to create muddy roads on which the exhausted soldiers would tread and be eaten alive by swarms of mosquitoes.

Both armies were reasonably close to each other, but neither side was quite sure where the other was located. Within a short time, however, the most protracted single battle of the war would begin.

There are several varying reports of who did what and how the battle proceeded. Nevertheless, most historians agree the fight was bloody, exhausting and appeared to be a draw, with neither side clearly able to claim a victory. Both sides fought bravely, but neither surrendered. It ended as the sun began setting and all the soldiers fell into unbelievable exhaustion.

The British decided to leave well enough alone and chose to secretly exit the area to reach Sandy Hook, where ships were waiting to bring them to New York City. By the next morning, some fourteen thousand British troops had marched along Kings Highway to Middletown. The next day, they continued their march down Linden Avenue in Highlands to Sandy Hook. Within a week, they would board barges that would bring them to the ships for safe transport to New York City.

And again, while there was no clear winner of this particular battle, it built tremendous confidence in the American troops themselves who had managed to go toe-to-toe with the most significant fighting force in the world, the dreaded redcoats.

Secondly, it made General George Washington a hero of not only his men but also the entire country. Those fellow officers and Patriot leaders who had been critical of Washington were now far more encouraged by his ability to lead.

STAY AWAY FROM PRISON SHIPS

These are the times that try men's souls.

—*Thomas Paine*

Almost every American prisoner was sent to a prison ship located either in Raritan Bay or in nearby Wallabout Bay (Brooklyn's Navy Yard, today) on the East River between New York City and Brooklyn.

The conditions on these ships were deplorable, and in many cases, prisoners died as a result of their incarceration. The British deliberately made the conditions of prison ships unbearable to encourage the American prisoners to join the British army.

More Americans died on these ships from deliberate neglect than the number of soldiers who died in every battle of the Revolution combined. You did not want to end up on a British prison ship under any circumstances.

More than eleven thousand men and women died from the overcrowding, contaminated water, starvation and disease aboard these ships. When they died, the British would bury their bodies along the shore. These were victims from all thirteen colonies and a variety of other countries.

SPIES AMONG US

George Washington knew the importance of obtaining reliable information about British intentions, locations and strategies during the war. Therefore, he personally designed a system of espionage to gain critical information from informants and spies. Both sides relied on spies for information.

For example, the "Spy House" in today's Port Monmouth, New Jersey—the Seabrook-Wilson House, built in 1648—was in cahoots with the Patriots.

British prison ship.

During the Revolutionary War, it was a tavern often visited by British troops. Remember, the troops didn't always have their own places to stay, eat or drink, and they frequently visited local establishments. The owner of this particular tavern overheard the British discuss their battle plans, and he passed along the information to the Patriots. He also kept track of the British ships in Raritan Bay and let the privateers know where they were anchored so they could row out to the described location by the dark of night to sabotage or attack a ship before quickly running back to one of the swamps or creeks flowing into Raritan Bay.

Another example is the Morgan Inn (later known as the Old Spye Inn), which was established in 1703 in the now Morgan section of Sayreville, New Jersey. The Morgan family had lived in the area for more than two hundred years, and many family members are buried in the privately owned Morgan Cemetery overlooking Raritan Bay. Many believed members of the Morgan family were related to the famous pirate Captain Henry Morgan, who visited the inn on several occasions.

Incidentally, following the Battle of Monmouth, Captain James Morgan, who also owned land in today's Sayreville, New Jersey, sent reconnaissance notes to "His Excelency Genriel Washanton [*sic*]" describing British

Seabrook-Wilson House.

activities in and on the shores of Raritan Bay. He wasn't a perfect speller. Within the Library of Congress, there are several illegible notes he wrote to Washington, such as this one, dated June 29, 1778: "Sir, this comes to inform you that a great quantity of small brigs and gunnery and boats came from New York and went into the Jersey Shore."

During the American Revolution, a local British Loyalist was captured by Continental army troops while trying to signal British ships in Raritan Bay. As a result, he was tried as a spy at the Morgan Inn, subsequently hanged from a nearby tree and then buried behind the inn in an unmarked grave. The inn was destroyed by fire in 1976, but the ruins are still listed in the National Register of Historic Places.

9

THE PATRIOTS AND LOYALISTS

UNLOVE THY NEIGHBOR

Love thy neighbor as thyself: Do not do to others what thou wouldst not wish be done to thyself: Forgive injuries. Forgive thy enemy, be reconciled to him, give him assistance, invoke God in his behalf.

—*Confucius*

Because New Jersey was located between New York and Philadelphia, it was strategically important for both the British and Continental armies. As a result, Monmouth County was a hotbed for conflict between Patriots and Loyalists. Fighting was so intense between these two politically motivated groups of citizens, it felt more like a civil war than a revolution.

Residents of Monmouth County and the counties surrounding them began choosing sides. About a third of the population aligned themselves with Great Britain. These were the Loyalists, and they were mostly the upper-crust folks, merchants and those who stood to gain financially from the outcome. Another third were Patriots in favor of independence from Great Britain. They were mostly farmers and those people who had a stake in gaining independence from the Mother Country. And then the final third of the population was independent, largely Quakers, who were pacifists.

Given the tension, it wasn't unusual for the local population to change sides if it kept them from harm from either dangerous neighbors or those who opposed them. The level of mistrust and fear in this area was intense. It truly was a hazardous environment in which to live or state your own political views. You might have been killed in the middle of the night as a result of your position. Therefore, most people avoided political discussion and kept their mouths mostly shut.

While the Continental army was fighting the redcoats, some of the Loyalists were fighting a clandestine war of intimidation with some of the Patriots. The Patriots were not only engaged in sabotage and murder but also secretly supplying the Continental army with whatever it needed.

GOVERNMENT-SANCTIONED PIRACY

When the American Revolution began, America had no warships to engage the English navy. Besides, America could not easily manufacture weapons. Much of the Continental army's weaponry was provided by those redcoats who died in battle and left their weapons in the fields to be picked up by Americans. In many ways, because Great Britain had the best trained and equipped army in the world, it's amazing we ever gained our independence. It took a different kind of fighting to wear down the Brits.

Because we had few military ships to do battle with the British navy, we began to repurpose more than two thousand merchant ships to defend ourselves. Collectively, these privately owned vessels were outfitted with more than eighteen thousand guns and some seventy thousand men, who were called privateers. In a sense, it was government-sanctioned piracy. Also, some of the American colonies developed their own navies to defend or attack hostile ships.

Eventually, General Washington did establish a naval force in 1775 to battle the British off the New England coast. He also authorized those privateers to help do damage to the British ships in whatever way they could.

We had become very good at hit-and-run tactics on land. Ambush the enemy and then run like the dickens into the woods and mountains. From there, we could easily disassemble our military groups so they could run back to their farms to hide until the next mission. Eventually, it became a game of cat-and-mouse, which the redcoats were not too adept at playing. But guerrilla warfare on land was not the only game we could play.

American warship.

We could terrorize the British in the local rivers and waterways by rowing whaleboats into Raritan Bay to wreak havoc on the British ships. After the damage was done, the privateers escaped back into the creeks, marshes and swamps along the bay, where the whaleboats would be hidden until another night.

For example, Pleasant Valley (present-day Marlboro) was well known by the British as the "Hornets' Nest" because it's where local Patriots would continually sting them by capturing and sinking ships in Sandy Hook Bay and then seizing Tories to exchange for American prisoners.

Privateering was often done under cover of darkness by smaller whaleboats, which carried small cannons. During daylight hours, these vessels could be hidden in the marshes or creeks that emptied into Raritan Bay. When the sun went down and the British were mostly sleeping, privateers would leave the creeks and wreak havoc on the British ships by firing a few shots into a ship's hull, stealing supplies or even capturing ships, if possible.

Privateering had become one of the most significant and effective military efforts in the entire war. In fact, by the end of the war, American privateers had seized some 1,500 British ships and captured more than 12,000 British sailors.

Our sustained privateering efforts in Raritan Bay, the Atlantic Ocean and other bays and rivers throughout the country did so much damage to both the private and military ships from England, it affected the attitude of British merchants, who were losing too many ships and products being shipped to America. British commerce was losing revenue while the cost of insurance skyrocketed. Eventually, the population who lived near Great Britain's coastline was becoming concerned about a potential attack from American privateers. British merchants were pushing against their own government to end the war.

THE "CORN KING" GETS STALKED

Make yourself sheep, and the wolves will eat you.
—Benjamin Franklin

Many Patriots helped privateers by providing them with whaleboats, weapons and supplies. They also helped them hide the boats during the day to ensure the boats would be available for more attacks on other nights. One such Patriot who rose to the occasion by not only supporting local efforts but also providing food to troops in New England was John Burrowes, who lived in Matawan (or Middletown Poynt as it was called at the time).

He was a prosperous grain merchant and quite wealthy. As a result of his huge success, everyone called him the Corn King. He would obtain grain from the locals, mill it in his own mills and then secretly ship it by boat to New England and New York City as a way to help the cause. He was a local hero, but there were spies everywhere and especially in Monmouth County, where nobody trusted anyone. And it was a safe bet that when someone like John Burrowes or his son, John Jr., helped fellow Patriots, more than a few people knew about it.

Members of the Burrowes family were truly Patriots who have become elevated to hero status as a result of their efforts during the Revolutionary War. They blatantly allowed the first militia group in Monmouth County to train in the front yard of their home in Matawan, New Jersey. Many of Loyalists thought the Burrowes family was asking for trouble.

Matawan was one of those communities, like many others, where neighbors were divided. And so it wasn't long before Burrowes's blatant loyalty to the

The Burrowes Mansion in Matawan, New Jersey. *Courtesy of New Jersey Historic Trust.*

Patriot cause was too much for the Loyalist sympathizers to stand. Eventually, it's why Loyalists raided the family home in Matawan in 1778.

These particular Loyalists were refugees who had lived in Sandy Hook and called themselves the "Greens." Whenever this group found an opportunity for vengeance against local Patriots, they would take it.

While John Jr. was visiting the family mansion in Matawan, the so-called Greens landed in Matawan Creek and headed toward the Burrowes home. Local Patriots, however, saw them coming and promptly warned the Burrowes family. As the Greens made their way to the house, John Jr. escaped out the back and swam across Matawan Creek to hide in the woods. The local Patriots began fighting with the Greens as soon as they arrived at the front of the house, but to no avail. The Greens had already set fire to the Burroweses' nearby mills and storehouses.

The Greens kicked in front door of the home at about midnight, but John Jr. was gone. His wife, however, came down the front stairs wearing a nightgown and shawl. One of the British soldiers demanded that she give up her shawl to wrap a wound on one of his soldiers. Margaret Burrowes refused. She said something in anger and was struck by the hilt of the soldier's sword as a reprimand. The Greens raced upstairs and searched the entire house. They even fired shots into the stairway, which can be seen today, but they found no one else.

Unfortunately, some Patriot militia were killed or captured during the raid. John Burrowes Sr. was also captured and released later on. Almost all of the furniture was brought to the front yard and burned as an example to those other Patriots in the neighborhood who might be watching.

Sadly, the Burrowes family fortune was destroyed as a result of the raid. The house was not harmed, however, and stands today in Matawan as a monument to this heroic family of the American Revolution.

A BAD BOY BECOMES A HERO

There are good people who are dealt a bad hand by fate, and bad people who live long, comfortable, privileged lives. A small twist of fate can save or end a life; random chance is a permanent, powerful player in each of our lives, and in human history as well.

—Jeff Greenfield

As conflict with Great Britain intensified to full-blown battle, another Patriot, Joshua Huddy, fell into the center ring of not just war but in the nasty business of neighbor against neighbor, Loyalists against Patriots. But this Patriot was far deadlier than any member of the Burrowes family.

The exploits of Joshua Huddy during the war frustrated British officials and the Loyalist population of central New Jersey beyond belief. They hated him, passionately, and eventually hanged him in Highlands, New Jersey. He was, in fact, the last person killed who was connected to the Revolutionary War. Oddly, his death occurred almost immediately after the war—after a peace treaty was signed with Great Britain.

Today, several places honor Huddy with memorials and plaques, such as Highlands, Toms River, Colts Neck and Rumson. But Huddy's life was complicated, and he frequently got into serious trouble. He certainly supported the need for war, but he was also capable of committing extreme acts of violence and cruelty even toward those closest to him.

It was hard to believe such a violent individual was born into a prosperous family in Salem County in southern New Jersey. However, despite his family's good standing, Joshua had always been in trouble, and eventually, he was kicked out of the Quakers for his "disorderly" conduct.

Huddy continued to be a bad boy for much of his life. He was convicted numerous times for assault and theft. He continually found himself in financial difficulty. As such, he had to eventually sell his family's plantation in Salem to pay his debts and was forced into debtor's prison for a time.

Before long, despite his rowdy ways, he married his first wife, who was a widow. Before his wife died, she gave birth to two daughters. Then he moved to Colts Neck in Monmouth County, where he married another widow, who happened to inherit Colts Neck Tavern.

Joshua Huddy (artistic representation).

The Monmouth County sheriff accused Huddy during a later time of trying to steal the tavern from his wife and then forcing her children to leave. It was typical behavior for Huddy, and so he often found himself in trouble with the law or in court.

Eventually, he made his way into prominence as the commander of an artillery company in the New Jersey Militia during 1777. Huddy's bad-boy attitude was perfect for his assigned job. Fellow Patriots thought he was an extremely aggressive commander in the militia. He had no sympathy toward anyone, even friends or neighbors who leaned toward the Loyalists. Most everyone feared him because of his reputation as a ruthless killer.

Eventually, Huddy's notoriety as a militia officer and privateer made him a target for Monmouth County Loyalists who wanted to punish him for his crimes.

WITH A NAME LIKE TITUS CORNELIUS

The moment the slave resolves that he will no longer be a slave, his fetters fall. Freedom and slavery are mental states.

—*Mahatma Gandhi*

More than eight thousand slaves worked in New Jersey, second only to the number of slaves working in New York.

Titus Cornelius (artistic representation).

Titus Cornelius, also known as Colonel Tye, was a slave brought from Africa to be "owned" by John Corlies, a Quaker with a farm located along the banks of the Navesink River near the town of Shrewsbury.

Quakers were pacifists and abhorred slavery. Nevertheless, Corlies owned slaves despite his faith. Generally, the Quakers taught slaves how to read and write. In some cases, they freed their slaves when they reached the age of twenty-one. But Corlies provided no education and absolutely no hope of any eventual freedom for any of his slaves. He was also tough on his slaves and would often whip them for minor infractions of the rules he set forth.

Even members of his own faith had admonished him for the treatment of his slaves. These Quakers also disapproved of his blatant refusal to provide his slaves with an education. Even after the Quakers officially forbade slavery in 1758, Corlies is said to have replied he had not thought it was his duty to give the slaves their freedom.

Meanwhile, despite his enslavement, Titus began to learn more about the political leanings of the nearby families in the area. Eventually, the Quakers revoked Corlies's membership as a Quaker because of his continuing refusal to free his slaves.

In 1775, the British-placed governor of Virginia issued a proclamation of which Titus soon became aware. It offered freedom to any slaves or indentured servants who escaped their masters and joined the British to fight in the war. The proclamation caused some 100,000 slaves in the region to conspire against their masters and join the British cause with the hope of becoming truly free.

Titus escaped from Corlies's property after the proclamation was made public. Soon, he was fighting in the British cause. When Corlies discovered Titus had fled, he advertised in local newspapers promising a reward of three pounds for the capture and return of Titus.

Assuming the adopted name of Tye, Cornelious enlisted first in the Ethiopian Regiment and fought in the Battle of Monmouth in 1778, where he demonstrated his ability as a soldier. Both sides were impressed. Later he gained prominence among the Loyalists when he captured a captain in the Monmouth militia and brought him to an infamous sugar house prison in New York City.

Tye unofficially called himself a colonel, even though the title was never formally recognized by the British. But his knowledge of the landscape in Monmouth County and his aggressive leadership provided him with the legitimacy he desired. He was not only well known for his efforts but also feared as a Loyalist guerrilla commander. As a result of his success, he was paid by the British to destabilize the region, which made the entire area a place where neighbors feared for their lives.

The plan to use guerrilla tactics was the brainchild of New Jersey's Royal Governor and Loyalist William Franklin. Remember him? He was Ben Franklin's son, and his plan was really an act of retaliation for the Patriot activities that led to the confiscation of Loyalist property. The final straw was reached when the Patriots of Monmouth County started hanging Tories under a convenient vigilante law.

One of Tye's most daring raids was in 1779, when he and some fifty African Americans captured eighty cattle, twenty horses and two well-known Patriots. Tye and his men were paid five gold guineas for their effort.

They often targeted wealthy slaveholding Patriots during their assaults, which frequently took place at night. He took prisoners and freed slaves if there were any. Often Tye would not only steal from Patriot families but also murder them and burn down their property. He could be vicious, and it's why so many people feared him.

After every raid, Tye and his fighters quickly made their way back to their base of operation in Sandy Hook. It was called Refugee Town, and they lived in tents and small structures that were just below and surrounding the lighthouse.

Before long, Colonel Tye began to serve with the Black Brigade, a group of two dozen black Loyalists. This group often worked together with an all-white Loyalist unit called the Queen's Rangers. The groups joined together to defend British-occupied New York City.

The Black Brigade also helped slaves escape and later assisted the same slaves with immigration to Nova Scotia for resettlement after the war had ended. The Patriots feared the Black Brigade even more than the regular British army because many of the former slaves knew precisely which homes belonged to the Patriots because they had been slaves there at one time.

CLASH OF THE TITANS

I beat him at his own game. I simply turned myself into a shark.
—Thetis, from the movie Clash of the Titans

At the start of the Revolutionary War, if you were an oddsmaker, you might very well favor the British to win the fight. After all, the British—beyond all doubt—had the best-equipped and best-trained army in the entire world.

While soldiers on both sides were fighting on the battlefields of New York and New Jersey, some Loyalists and Patriots were fighting up close and personal.

So, too, both Colonel Tye (Loyalist) and Captain Joshua Huddy (Patriot) were each fighting with a purpose in mind. Each thought his cause was the just cause.

Almost everyone feared Colonel Tye and Captain Joshua Huddy. And each thought they would win in the end. They both had much more in common, however, than they realized. They shared a mutual destiny, and in 1780, they would meet face to face.

It was in the middle of the night in Colts Neck, New Jersey, when Colonel Tye led a small group of African Americans and Queen's Rangers to raid the home of Captain Joshua Huddy. Huddy was in his house next to the Colt's Neck Inn. According to a well-documented account of the attack, Huddy and an African American servant, Lucretia Emmons, were in the house alone as Colonel Tye's band of Loyalists began firing their muskets.

Incidentally, Huddy had allowed his house to be used for the storage of an extensive collection of stolen muskets, which were provided to the militia

Home of Joshua Huddy.

as needed. As a result, Huddy and his companion had lots of guns and ammunition for just two people.

If there's any humor to be realized from this horrific attack, it's this:

Huddy and his servant were able to hold off Colonel Tye's siege on the house for almost two hours by Huddy running from window to window and firing a musket toward the outside as the servant girl reloaded musket after musket right behind him, giving the illusion to anyone attacking that there were more than just two people inside. It was a remarkably creative strategy that appeared to be working until Tye gave the orders to burn down the house.

As Huddy realized his ploy would no longer work, he ran outside to surrender and to request that the fire be put out so that his house could be spared from destruction. Some historians say the Loyalists obliged his request while others write that they were so upset about being fooled they let the house burn to the ground. Huddy's slave girl, Emmons, who some say was also his girlfriend, managed to escape. Some historians report Huddy's home had survived the fire but was later torn down in 1842. Today, there's a historic sign in Colts Neck marking the site of the house.

Huddy was in handcuffs and surrounded by Loyalists. He was led from his house next to Colt's Neck Inn to a place called Black Point, which is today's Rumson. It's where the Navesink River joins the Shrewsbury River. Black Point was a strategic location because it was next to an inlet leading to the Atlantic Ocean that no longer exists today. Interestingly, during this period, the Navesink River flowed directly into the Atlantic Ocean, where

Black Point in Rumson, New Jersey.

a British ship was waiting to take Huddy across Raritan Bay and into New York Harbor to a prison in British-held New York City.

Coincidentally, there was a battle at Black Point just one year earlier in 1779 in the same area where the British were trying to leave in a boat with Huddy. This battle started when a British raiding party marched from Tinton Falls to Black Point. While they were trying to embark from Black Point, they were attacked by a detachment of the Continental army. Eleven Americans were killed or wounded. The battle ended when a flag of truce was flown, and both sides walked away.

THE GREAT ESCAPE

By the will art thou lost, by the will art thou found, by the will art thou free, captive, and bound.

—*Angelus Silesius (1624–1677)*

So now, back to our story. Colonel Tye was trying to embark on a boat to deliver Joshua Huddy to a ship in the Atlantic Ocean that would carry him to prison in New York City.

However, the Monmouth County Militia got wind of the capture and followed closely behind Colonel Tye until reaching Black Point. When

Huddy was placed on a boat to begin his voyage to captivity, the militia began its assault on Huddy's captors.

During the encounter, the boat overturned in the swift current where the Navesink Estuary entered the Shrewsbury River. Six Loyalists were killed, and Colonel Tye was wounded in the wrist. Later, Tye would die from this wound after it became infected with tetanus. Because Huddy was not clearly seen or because muskets were never that accurate, he was shot in the hip by friendly fire, presumably, as he tried escaping to the shoreline.

Huddy's injury forced him to stay in hiding for several months while his wound healed. Then, in 1781, Huddy's bravery in escaping from the British at Black Point was rewarded with an important assignment: command of a blockhouse in Toms River and guarding the local saltworks. Salt was an essential commodity to both sides. For the most part, it was used to keep meat from spoiling. A blockhouse in those days was a fortification in which the people inside of it could fire in all directions.

A year later, Huddy was confronted at the blockhouse in Toms River by a large group of both British and Loyalist troops who eventually burned down the village of Toms River. Huddy surrendered because he and his men had run out of gunpowder to defend themselves. He was immediately taken to a notorious sugar house prison in New York City on a whaleboat. I'll explain Huddy's fate, but first a bit about William Franklin, who also plays a role in this story.

FAMOUS FATHER AND INFAMOUS SON

If you intend to set the colonies aflame, take care to run away by the light of it.
—*William Franklin*

Meanwhile, Benjamin Franklin's son, William Franklin, had been the last royal governor of New Jersey before the Patriots had arrested him for siding with the British. Remember, if you will, Ben was a Patriot, while his son, William, was a Loyalist.

As the proponents of independence grew more substantial, a governing body was formed in New Jersey to supersede the authority of the royal governor. It was called the Provincial Congress of New Jersey, and in 1776, its members ordered William Franklin to be placed under house arrest at Proprietary House in Perth Amboy. He remained under house arrest with

Proprietary House in Perth Amboy, New Jersey.

his wife, Elizabeth, for five months while the Revolutionary War continued and the United States moved closer to declaring independence.

While under house arrest, William Franklin tried to reassert his power by calling on the New Jersey Assembly to meet with him. A representative of the Provincial Congress of New Jersey met with William Franklin and presented him with an option. He could be officially arrested and sent to prison, or if he agreed to step down from the governorship, he could leave Perth Amboy to stay peaceably at Princeton, Bordentown or at a farm property William owned in Willingboro, New Jersey.

William refused to agree with stepping down as governor, so he was promptly arrested. William's wife was left behind at the Proprietary House, where she lived for another year, but she never saw her husband again.

After a hearing, the Continental Congress decided William Franklin should be removed from New Jersey and taken to a prison in Connecticut. Nine days later, the Declaration of Independence was ratified and adopted by the Continental Congress, which ironically included William's father, Benjamin Franklin.

FRANKLIN'S REVENGE

The alternate domination of one faction over another, sharpened by the spirit of revenge natural to party dissension, which in different ages and countries has perpetrated the most horrid enormities, is itself a frightful despotism. But this leads at length to a more formal and permanent despotism.
— *General George Washington*

William was held as a prisoner in Connecticut until 1778. His wife had left the Proprietary House to live in British-occupied New York City, where she died shortly after that.

When Franklin was released from prison, he moved to New York City, where he became the primary leader of the Loyalists and organized military units to fight on the British side. He knew all about Joshua Huddy and hated him.

Joshua Huddy leaving prison to be hanged.

Last Will and Testament of Joshua Huddy. *Courtesy of Michael Kovic.*

Huddy had just been captured in Toms River and brought to Sugar House Prison in lower Manhattan. However, William Franklin convinced the British authorities to release Huddy from the prison in New York City so he could be used as a bargaining chip in an exchange of prisoners. That's what Franklin told everyone, but his intention was far more deadly. There would be no prisoner exchange.

Instead, Huddy was summarily removed from the prison and sent to Highlands, New Jersey, where Franklin intended to hang him in revenge for the murders of Loyalists. On April 12, 1782, Joshua Huddy arrived under guard in a section of Highlands called Gravelly Point. Before he was executed, in what today is Huddy Park, they allowed him to dictate and sign his will. He gave all his possessions to his two daughters. And then it was over.

When Huddy's body was found and recovered by the Patriot forces the next day, they read a sign attached to him: "We, the Refugees, having long with the grief beheld the cruel murders of our brethren…determined not to suffer without taking vengeance…and thus begin, having made Captain

Huddy as the first object to present to your view; and we further determine to hang man for man while there is a Refuge existing....Up goes Huddy for Philip White." White was one of the Loyalists Huddy was accused of murdering.

Captain Lippincott, who coordinated the hanging of Joshua Huddy, was given three thousand acres of land in Canada after the war by the British for remaining loyal. Although Lippincott fought for the British, he was from Monmouth County and was born in Shrewsbury. When William Franklin was released in a prisoner exchange with the British in 1778, he then went to British-occupied New York City, where he would spend the rest of the war. After the war ended, he moved to Britain, where he lived the rest of his life.

OUR FIRST INTERNATIONAL INCIDENT

The weak can never forgive. Forgiveness is the attribute of the strong.
—*Mahatma Gandhi*

General Washington's troops (militia and regulars) were outraged with the hanging of Joshua Huddy and demanded retaliation for what they perceived as an act of murder and not an act of war.

Washington declared that if the individual responsible for Huddy's death were not turned over to the Continentals, a British captain would be chosen at random among the prisoners of war and executed.

Less than two months after the hanging of Huddy, British captain Charles Asgill was selected in a drawing to be the one punished as revenge.

Eventually, Washington and members of Congress determined that executing Asgill would result in more unnecessary violence by both sides. And besides, everyone knew the Revolutionary War was coming to an end. But Washington needed to save face with his troops who wanted revenge. As a result, the French foreign minister helped Washington and Congress by publicly appealing for a stay of execution for Asgill. Congress agreed, gladly. And it was over.

Later, British general Henry Clinton wrote to General Washington calling the execution of Captain Joshua Huddy an "act of barbarity." Oddly, Huddy was one of only two American prisoners of war executed by the British during the American Revolution.

Captain Charles Asgill. *Thomas Philips.*

Huddy was buried in an unknown location on the grounds of Old Tennent Church in Manalapan Township in New Jersey, where a simple military marker sits near the church itself. More than four hundred people attended his funeral service.

Huddy's contributions to the Patriot cause in present-day Monmouth and Ocean Counties are commemorated in several monuments and parks named for him. And while his methods of terroristic intimidation and murder among communities of Loyalists seem barbaric, he remains a hero of the American Revolution.

Benjamin Franklin and his son, William, saw each other one time after the Revolutionary War came to an end. They met in London in 1785 to sort out some business and financial matters. After the strictly business meeting, the two men never spoke again. Benjamin died in Philadelphia five years after meeting with his son, who died in London in 1813.

10

THE WINNERS

WHAT IN THE WORLD JUST HAPPENED?

I shall constantly bear in Mind, that as the Sword was the last Resort for the preservation of our Liberties, so it ought to be the first thing laid aside, when those Liberties are firmly established.

—*General George Washington*

Looking back over the centuries, how could the colonists honestly believe in their abilities to fight against the best army in the world? How could America be serious about fighting with proverbial sticks and stones against a well-fortified and well-trained army? It took a whole lot of gumption.

The conflict lasted a total of seven years, with the significant American victory at Yorktown, Virginia, in 1781, marking the end of hostilities. The Treaty of Paris was signed two years later in 1783, officially ending the conflict.

Historians and scholars surmise the British never had a strategy for winning the war. Some go further and say even if the war had been won by the British, the English generals were reluctant to own the spoils of war.

So the British chose to take limited risks, and it wasn't the wisest decision they could make. Also, the war was becoming far more costly than ever anticipated. Even resupplying the troops with ships from abroad took time, and England had enough to worry about back home.

General George Washington at Trenton, 1792. *John Trumbull.*

But probably more important than any of these considerations was that the British overestimated the support from the Loyalists, which they dearly needed to win. The Loyalists were perceived as never really stepping up to the plate to fully commit themselves to supporting the British cause.

And perhaps the role of the Patriots, mostly in Monmouth County, New Jersey, was more critical to winning the war than anyone thought at the time or realized in the present. Patriots, like Burrowes and Huddy and so many more, really did ignite the engine to move a young country forward.

HELLO, GOODBYE

When the British finally left in 1783, they took along many of the Loyalists, including prominent people in business, lawyers, financiers and clergymen.

The Anglican Church had been especially influential in the colonial era, and it began to lose much of its influence as many of its members also departed. It also lost its funding from the British Society for the Propagation of the Gospel and was eventually abolished in 1784. As a result, it also lost control of King's College, which is now Columbia University. And New York City became more democratic and much more open to ambitious entrepreneurs from middle-class and poor backgrounds.

As the British retreated, tens of thousands of Loyalists left America to escape the dangerous world in which they would be ridiculed or even killed for their political beliefs. About half of the Loyalists returned to Great Britain. The rest went to Canada to settle in Nova Scotia and New Brunswick.

But the British also have a kind of complicated relationship to the Loyalists because the British have a complicated relationship to the Revolutionary War and to the United States, a place that they wanted and failed to hold on to. And the Loyalists were, at times, an uneasy reminder of this defeat.

In the end, the story of America's fight for independence is complicated and far beyond what several thousand words or even a single book can describe adequately. But hopefully, you at least have a better understanding of what contribution this part of the United States made to the collective effort.

NOT SO FAST

While most of the British troops left New York City and sailed home to England, there were still a few ships of the Royal Navy that had not pulled up anchor quite yet. One of England's warships, the HMS *Assistance*, was preparing to depart on December 30, 1783, but had sent five sailors ashore at Sandy Hook to get fresh water before they set sail. Guess what? These individuals decided to desert the ship and stay in America instead of getting water.

The next day, six more crew members also deserted. The ship's commander sent a search party of fourteen men ashore to find the eleven deserters in frigid weather. Then it started to snow for two days, and the crew members still hadn't returned to the ship. The ship's commander, Hamilton Douglas Halyburton, and additional crew members went ashore for one last look. The next day, more crew members went looking and found the commander and search parties frozen to death in the snow. They were buried at Sandy Hook on the following day. The deserters, however, were never found.

After the commander's death on Sandy Hook, his mother, Katherine, had a marble monument erected at the site of the graves with a plaque that read:

Here lie the remains of the Honorable Hamilton Douglass Haliburton, son of Shoto Charles, Earl of Morton, and heir of the ancient family of Haliburton, of Pitcurr in Scotland, who perished on this coast, with twelve more young gentlemen and one common sailor, in the spirited discharge of duty, the 30th or 31st of December, 1783—born October the 10th, 1763: a youth who in contempt of hardship and danger, though possessed of an ample fortune, served seven years in the British navy, with a manly courage. He seemed to be deserving of a better fate. To his dear memory, and that of his unfortunate companions, this monumental stone is erected, by his unhappy mother, Katherine Countess Dowager of Morton.

In 1808, a French ship landed off Sandy Hook, and because France was at war with the British, the crew destroyed the monument. As a result, the graves were unmarked and forgotten. In 1908, however, the remains of the fourteen sailors were discovered while workers were digging, and the bodies were exhumed and then interred at a cemetery in Brooklyn.

Another monument was built in 1937 at the same location as the original monument. Two years later, Queen Elizabeth and King George VI of England visited the United States to pay their respects at the second monument.

Eventually, the last of the British ships had left America in defeat by the end of 1783.

ON OUR OWN AT LAST

We should not look back unless it is to derive useful lessons from past errors, and for the purpose of profiting by dearly bought experience.
—*George Washington*

By the time we did gain our independence in 1783, the fortifications along our seacoasts were in deplorable condition. A decade after winning the war against England, we were now becoming increasingly concerned about a potential conflict in Europe. As a result, we built twenty forts at thirteen harbors throughout the United States.

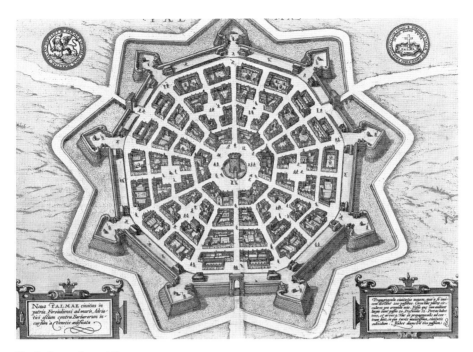

Typical star-shaped fort.

These forts were relatively small and consisted of walls laid out at angles resembling a star shape so that the enemy could not gather at the bottom of a particular wall beneath a vertical field of fire. In this way, those defending any of the walls could clearly see and then fire at the enemy near the base of the adjacent walls. A single tier of cannons was usually on the roof of the fort. The first of the forts were built in Portsmouth, New Hampshire; Boston, Massachusetts; Newport, Rhode Island; Philadelphia, Pennsylvania.

Now young America was on its own, and life was rough. Infants often died young. If someone got sick, there was a good chance they could die.

Even though many people were religious, most were superstitious.

Most people either worked on a farm or owned one. Believe it or not, poverty was not prevalent compared to England at the time.

Plantations were owned by wealthy landowners who used slaves of African descent. Wealthy women also owned slaves to help them with their household chores.

For the most part, boys received an education while girls were raised to be responsible for household duties. Many wealthy citizens could afford to attend college.

Women, slaves and poor men could not vote and could not hold any public office. Middle-class men were able to vote, but they usually didn't aspire to hold any political position. The wealthiest men, however, held most of the political power. As you might imagine, men were in charge.

Men and women were marrying quite young. If you were a widow or widower, you remarried quite quickly. Folks were not divorcing because it was virtually unknown as an option for an unhappy marriage. Religion also made it quite clear that marriage was forever.

Lots of married couples had large families. Parents and grandparents of these families would live with them.

Poor people made their clothing for the most part. The wealthy could afford to have custom clothing made, or they could purchase clothing from stores.

There was plenty of food in those days, but the variety was somewhat limited. Most of the food was grown and cooked at home.

Medicine had not progressed enough to do much good. There weren't many doctors, and those who existed weren't well trained. Society took a dim view of their collective abilities.

The type of house you lived in depended on your wealth. Homes were not electrified and were heated by a fireplace. There was no plumbing, and you either had an outhouse or you visited the backyard or woods to do your business. The most common type of home was the log cabin because it didn't require refined lumber to build.

If you had indentured servants, they would serve five to seven years. Let's be truthful, however. They were considered slaves and were not paid. They were not allowed to get married.

Wealthy entrepreneurs primarily invested in land and commercial opportunities.

There weren't many roads, so transportation was limited to walking or to riding a horse on dirt paths. The preferred method of travel, however, was via the waterways leading to Raritan Bay.

The good news is that mail delivery and newspapers were available, but not quite regularly or timely.

Men would usually hunt and entertain themselves with participating, viewing and betting on cockfights in which enraged roosters would fight each other, often until death. Women participated in less violent activities, such as sewing and quilting. Both men and women loved music and dancing. Religion was also firmly embedded in American society during these days. People said their daily prayers and attended church on Sundays, where the rich people sat in the front and the poor sat in the back.

The entire area surrounding Raritan Bay began developing quickly. There was a growing feeling of independence among some, but the island of Manhattan was very definitely split in its loyalties to the king. Remember, the city was under British occupation until the end of the war and was the last port from which British ships sailed back home in 1783.

New York City, however, was somewhat cosmopolitan even from the beginning. A visitor to the city during the early revolutionary period wrote that "the inhabitants are in general brisk and lively" and the women were "handsome"—as did others new to the city—though, he added, "it rather hurts a European eye to see so many Negro slaves upon the streets."

Freedom of worship was an integral part of the city's values because of the 1735 libel trial of John Peter Zenger, editor of the *New-York Weekly Journal*. His innocence had established the principle of freedom of the press.

A fresh new America was starting to get its feet on the ground.

11

THE PLANNERS

GETTING TERRITORIAL

Only to the white man was nature a wilderness and only to him was the land "infested" with "wild" animals and "savage" people. To us it was tame, Earth was bountiful and we were surrounded with the blessings of the Great Mystery.

—*Black Elk, Oglala Lakota Sioux*

In 1787, New Jersey became the third state to ratify the U.S. Constitution and the first to sign the Bill of Rights.

New York City became the national capital under the Articles of Confederation from 1785 to 1789 and then briefly served as the new nation's capital from 1789 to 1790 under the United States Constitution. Under the new government, the City of New York hosted George Washington's inauguration as the first president of the United States, the drafting of the Bill of Rights and the first Supreme Court of the United States.

By 1790, Trenton had officially become the state capital of New Jersey.

In 1915, historian Paul Haworth wrote about a fishing trip George Washington took in 1790 that was described in a local newspaper:

Yesterday afternoon, the President of the United States returned from Sandy Hook, and the fishing banks, where he had been for the benefit of sea, air, and to amuse himself in the delightful recreation of fishing. We are told he has had excellent sport, having himself caught a great number of sea-bass and black fish—the weather proved remarkably fine, which, together with the salubrity of the air and wholesome exercise, rendered this little voyage extremely agreeable.

When the Revolutionary War ended, America entered a period known as Territorial Expansion, when the country was organized into territories and then states. The first most significant expansion was the Louisiana Purchase of 1803, which effectively doubled the country's territory.

New Jersey and New York grew and prospered during the early 1800s. New factories sprang up throughout both states. Paterson became a textile center and then later became known for producing trains and silk. Trenton was turning out clay products, iron and steel. Camden, Elizabeth, Jersey City, Newark and Passaic all became important manufacturing centers in the 1800s.

Along Raritan Bay, an English landowner named Richard Hartshorne owned a great deal of property he had purchased from the Lenape natives. In 1806, he transferred some of his property on northern Sandy Hook to the federal government for military use.

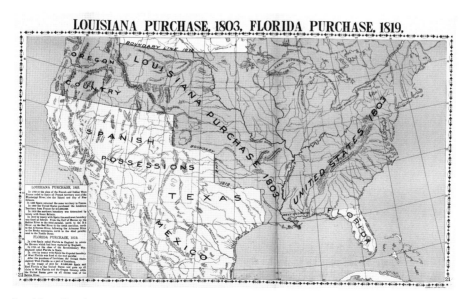

Louisiana Purchase of 1803. *Library of Congress.*

In 1807, President Thomas Jefferson was concerned about a possible war with Great Britain once more so the defense of America's coastal areas was a significant concern for our country.

Before airplanes were developed, we were merely concerned about enemies approaching our shores by ships. We'd have lots of tall lookout structures with telescopes and binoculars to scan the horizon for anything headed our way.

We also created forts to protect our major harbors, such as New York. A French engineer had developed the concept of protecting a fort's guns by enclosing the weapons in a casemate with an opening for the gun itself. Therefore, Castle Williams on Governor's Island in New York Harbor was built with casemates.

It was far more economical to build defensive structures than sending armies or a navy across the ocean to fight battles. During this period of construction, the U.S. Army Corps of Engineers was responsible for constructing these so-called fixed defenses. Regardless of our efforts, we were not very well prepared for the upcoming War of 1812.

THE BRASH BRITS

Were you to read the British press today, you would learn that the British Empire never forgets its defeats.
—*Robert Trout, broadcast news reporter*

Almost thirty years after the end of the Revolutionary War, the British were back for revenge—perhaps.

By the early 1800s, the British were routinely kidnapping American seamen who were aboard merchant vessels and forcing them to serve in the British navy (called impressment). There were hundreds of British ships off the coast, such as near New York Harbor and Sandy Hook, New Jersey.

In one particular instance in 1804, the British pulled next to an American ship and impressed (kidnapped without ransom) Thomas Cook of Shrewsbury, New Jersey. During this incident, three other British warships were anchored near Sandy Hook. One thing led to another, and someone got nervous and fired on an American ship within our territorial waters right off the coast of New Jersey. And if that wasn't bad enough, another British warship started firing on another American ship near Sandy Hook and yet another boat about a mile from the beaches of the Jersey shore.

Passengers on one of the American ships said later that the British climbed aboard and took all of the male passengers, both boys and men. Seventeen of them were impressed into service with the Royal Navy. Here's a quote from someone on board that day: The male passengers were "torn from their mothers, wives, and sisters, who were left in distress that cannot be described."

British warships were taking Americans within three miles of the coast of Monmouth County. In 1806, a British ship opened fire on an American trading sloop. An American, John Pierce, was killed within sight of the New Jersey shore, and residents of both New York and New Jersey were inflamed with anger.

The British consul in New York at long last realized his country's actions were not so good. The American public perceived the British violations of America's neutral rights as a violation of American sovereignty. Period.

The British were not only seizing American ships and sailors but also supporting Native American resistance against a young America. Was this revenge for the Revolution? Not sure, but one thing for certain was we would not tolerate British insults to our honor.

Looking back at the War of 1812, it's not always clear why the fight began. There were so many moving parts in so many areas involving so many different people, and it's difficult to know where to start in describing it.

A whole bunch of people opposed the war because they thought it just might interfere with our trade agreements with England, which many folks in this country depended on. In the end, we didn't have much of a choice, so Congress authorized the president to declare war against Britain in 1812.

In a somewhat strange move, America tried to seize parts of Canada, thinking it might bring about British concessions regarding our mutual relationships with Indians.

Sorry to say our army was not entirely organized well enough, and it was poorly equipped. Oh, by the way, the army was also somewhat small. Nevertheless, we chalked up two victories against our dear friends, the Brits. One win was near Lake Erie in 1813, while the other was in a battle in which American Indian resistance was virtually eliminated. It would be the last time the British tried to build a so-called buffer between the United States and Canada.

When the United States first declared war on Great Britain, the U.S. Navy had a few ships, while the Royal Navy had more than five hundred warships. Eighty-five of those British ships were in American waters when the war started.

The British also outmatched us in numbers of military personnel with 140,000 seamen. We had some 5,000 seamen.

Most of America's seven million people lived in coastal states, and for more than a century, seafaring had been both a livelihood and a lifeline in North America. This way of life was threatened when the British, exercising their advantage, established a blockade along the Eastern Seaboard, strangling American shipping and commerce.

While we're dealing with the war, Europe also had some influence on our battle with the British. When Napoleon abdicated in 1814, the British were able to focus more fully on us. Great. What did the British do? They plundered and burned Washington, D.C., including the White House. Then they tried to capture Baltimore in the Battle of Fort McHenry, during which Francis Scott Key penned the poem that would later become the U.S. national anthem, "The Star-Spangled Banner." Luckily, they failed to take the city.

Long story short, by 1815, the conflict with the British appeared to be at a stalemate, so we entered into peace negotiations with our dear British friends. The Treaty of Ghent formally ended the war. A lot of folks around the world seemed to be impressed with our ability to once again go toe-to-toe with Merry Old England.

For the American Indians, the war was not so good. General Andrew Jackson destroyed the military capabilities of many Indians during the Battle of Horseshoe Bend. The death of Tecumseh ended any prospect of a Native American alliance, as the British essentially abandoned their Native American allies. With no protection from the British and very little tribal cohesion, Native Americans would suffer further defeats as the United States continued to expand ever westward.

DEVELOPING DEFENSES

The principle of self-defense, even involving weapons and bloodshed, has never been condemned, even by Gandhi.

—Martin Luther King Jr.

While the War of 1812 provided us with some degree of confidence in our ability to defend ourselves, it also stimulated our sense of being vulnerable to attack by foreign nations and forced us to analyze our defenses.

As a result, recommendations were made to construct a sizeable permanent fortification at the end of Sandy Hook, but it wasn't until just before the Civil War that work was started on the fort. It was a wooden fortification called Fort Gates, but it was never completed and was deserted after the Civil War.

Meanwhile, new canals and railroads helped our industries grow. Europeans started coming by the thousands to New Jersey and New York to work in the factories. The opening of the Erie Canal provided excellent steamboat connections to upstate New York and the Great Lakes, along with coastal traffic to lower New England, making New York City the preeminent port to access the Atlantic Ocean. The arrival of rail connections to the north and west in the 1840s and 1850s strengthened its central role.

South Jersey remained rural for the most part, growing crops to feed the urban areas nearby. Railroads were essential in helping the South Jersey seashore areas expand.

During the next three years, a large wharf was constructed on Sandy Hook that could receive new building supplies and materials as the fortification of another fort was laid out.

What also followed after the Revolutionary War and the War of 1812 was a tremendous growth spurt of evolution in moving the country farther and farther west until we had access to the Pacific Ocean. But we weren't finished with war by any stretch. In 1845, the annexation of the Republic of Texas caused our war with Mexico and led to our acquisition of the northern half of Mexico's territory, which became real estate in California.

12

THE SLAVES

SLAVERY AND THE CIVIL WAR

Not only do I pray for it, on the score of human dignity, but I can clearly foresee that nothing but the rooting out of slavery can perpetuate the existence of our union, by consolidating it in a common bond of principle.
—*George Washington*

Building a new country with an infrastructure to support it was not only costly but also demanded an incredibly large workforce. One way this need for workers could be addressed was through immigration. The other way was through slavery. And because the country was pushing westward, the new territories were looking at the southern states as a model for how they could conquer the rough and dangerous landscape.

Meanwhile, many poor English and Dutch immigrants also entered the country as indentured servants who would work for many years to repay the cost of their travel to America. Soon, however, many indentured servants returned to England, and before long, the colonists in New Jersey were looking elsewhere for free labor. They looked to Africa for slaves.

Slavery in and around Raritan Bay had started in New York City with the Dutch. The Dutch West India Company brought about a dozen slaves to New Amsterdam in 1626. Less than twenty-five years later, the first full-fledged slave auctions were being held, and by the early 1700s, almost half of the houses and businesses in today's Manhattan were purchasing slaves to be both domestic servants and workers. New Amsterdam was second only to Charleston, South Carolina, for having the most slaves of any towns in all the colonies. Slaves were also being used to work in many jobs in and outside the island city. They also worked on farms in Long Island and elsewhere in the state.

New Jersey also depended on slaves to do much of the work in building the colony. Bergen County quickly became one of the largest counties with slaves because of the jobs required in its ports near the Hackensack and Passaic Rivers, which flowed into Newark Bay, Arthur Kill and Kill van Kull leading to New York Harbor.

During the time of the Revolutionary War, the British were occupying New York City and had urged the slaves to leave their masters and seek refuge in Manhattan. So, sure enough, more than ten thousand slaves had run to New York by 1780. They came from the North and South.

The Underground Railroad had several routes crossing New Jersey that were familiar to those slaves trying to escape to freedom. Several of the routes went to Jersey City, where slaves could cross the Hudson River and find their way to the British stronghold of Manhattan.

Unfortunately, when the war had concluded, the British helped only about three thousand slaves evacuate from New York to Nova Scotia, where they could resettle. To the Patriots, they were disdained as "Black Loyalists."

After the Revolutionary War, many of the northern states began passing laws that abolished slavery. New Jersey, however, did not abolish slavery until 1804. In New York, all slaves were eventually emancipated by 1840.

Oddly, the last sixteen slaves in New Jersey were not provided with their freedom until 1865 and only because the Thirteenth Amendment of the Constitution required it as follows: "Neither slavery nor involuntary servitude, except as a punishment for crime whereof the party shall have been duly convicted, shall exist within the United States, or any place subject to their jurisdiction."

Then along came the American Civil War in 1861; the fighting was mostly about slavery. Now bear in mind, when the War Between the States began, the so-called United States comprised thirty-four individual states. However, seven of those thirty-four decided to secede from the country to become the Confederate States of America.

These rebellious states were never diplomatically recognized by the United States government, nor were they acknowledged by any foreign country. As you probably know, those states remaining loyal to the federal government became known as the Union.

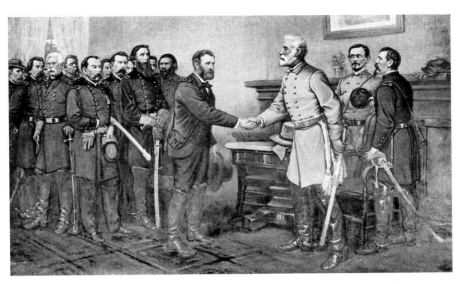

Grant accepts Lee's surrender. *Reproduction of a painting by Thomas Nast, completed thirty years after the surrender.*

Both sides, the Union and the Confederacy, quickly raised both volunteer and conscription armies. The battles were mostly fought in Confederate territory, or the South. During the four years of war between the two entities, up to 750,000 people were killed. This was more than the total number of dead soldiers in all military conflicts up until then.

Finally, the war was over on April 9, 1865, when General Robert E. Lee surrendered to General Ulysses S. Grant at the Appomattox Court House. Again, because most of the battles were contained in Confederate territory, most of the South's infrastructure was obliterated, especially the railroads and other means of transportation. The end of the war resulted in the collapse of the Confederacy and the abolishment of slavery, with four million slaves freed as a result.

The Civil War did not dramatically affect New York and New Jersey. No battles took place within the states at any time during the war, but New Jersey soldiers participated in almost every major eastern battle. New Jersey provided some ninety thousand soldiers and thirty regiments (groups of soldiers), including cavalry (soldiers on horseback) and infantry (soldiers on foot).

New York also became a primary source of troops, supplies, equipment and financing for the Union army. The state provided more than 450,000 soldiers during the war, of which more than 130,000 were foreign-born, including 20,000 from British possessions such as Canada. Some 51,000 were Irish and 37,000 German.

Oddly, at the end of the Civil War and when slavery was finally abolished, New Jersey still thought it needed slaves, so it was the last state to adopt the law against slavery.

The war had been costly, but we did learn several valuable lessons about fighting, fortifications and, most importantly, the need for better weapons. The military suddenly realized that the guns and fortifications used during the Civil War were fast becoming obsolete. Firing cannonballs was becoming an utterly antiquated way to direct projectiles. As a result, the country focused on developing new weaponry and fortifications that could better defend the nation from an advancing enemy presumably from Europe.

13

THE WEAPONS

BUILDING FORTIFICATIONS

*If you entrench yourself behind strong fortifications, you compel the enemy
seek a solution elsewhere.*
— *Carl von Clausewitz*

The year 1890 found the world at a tremendous scientific crossroad.
Because steam now powered the steel warships of many larger foreign
countries' navies—especially those of Great Britain, France, Germany and
Spain—the United States began feeling more vulnerable to attack than
ever before. The foreign policy of the United States was one of isolation,
and no modern navy would be built to match the fleets that were now
taking shape across the Atlantic. As a result, construction of a major fort
at Sandy Hook began.

Sandy Hook, New Jersey, was no stranger to fortifications. It had
been armed to repel naval attack during both the American Revolution
and the War of 1812. A third-generation fort at Sandy Hook had been
designed in the late 1840s by then-captain Robert E. Lee of the Army
Corps of Engineers, who created it before the War Between the States
began. Yes, this was the very same person who would lead the Army of
Northern Virginia and who surrendered to General Ulysses S. Grant to
end the Civil War.

Partially completed fort on Sandy Hook, New Jersey. *Photograph by Thomas Smedley.*

The fort was designed as a five-bastion irregular pentagon with 173 fixed guns facing toward three different areas in the Atlantic Ocean, New York Harbor and Sandy Hook Bay. Another 39 guns were to face south, covering the landward approaches.

Unfortunately, advancements in weaponry were moving too quickly, and we discovered masonry forts were vulnerable to the newer rifled guns. Construction slowed during the Civil War, and funding for stone fortifications abruptly stopped in 1867, so the fort remained incomplete. By 1885, the stone walls were cannibalized to help build the Sandy Hook Proving Ground's supporting structures, such as a new seawall.

Today, a small section of the granite wall, with three casemates, may still be seen buried deep in the woods in front of the chain-linked and barbed-wire fence of the Sandy Hook Coast Guard Station. A larger portion, the southwest bastion of the fort, was repurposed in the 1890s to support a water tower, so visitors to Sandy Hook may still see it today.

With traditional fortifications of brick and stone now obsolete, America found itself more vulnerable than ever before. Modern fleets from other countries were on the seas, but there was no modern U.S. Navy to attack them or modern fortifications to defend from them. A new system of fortifications was needed and needed quickly.

By 1890, the army began constructing the first of many concrete gun batteries, which could be aimed toward approaching enemy ships coming

Today's view of a portion of the Old Fort on Sandy Hook.

our way. By 1895, the army renamed the fortifications at Sandy Hook as Fort Winfield Scott Hancock, which would protect New York Harbor from invasion by sea. Its yellow-brick buildings were constructed mostly between 1898 and 1910.

As Fort Hancock was being constructed, other existing forts located in the major port cities of our country were being modernized, and new ones were also being built during the next ten years to augment our overall defenses.

Fort Wadsworth, with its existing Civil War–era fortification Battery Weed, and Fort Tompkins at the Narrows on Staten Island, New York, was supplemented with the new types of concrete batteries and rifled guns. Another existing fort, Fort Hamilton, on the Brooklyn side of the Narrows, received similar modernization. Along with Fort Hancock, these three locations covered the ocean approaches to New York, as well as the lower harbor. Fort Jay, dating from the late 1700s, was retained for administration purposes on Governor's Island within New York Harbor.

The eastern approaches to New York City were defended at Throgs Neck, where the East River empties into Long Island Sound. Civil War–era defenses such as Forts Schuyler in the Bronx and Fort Totten in Queens were also modernized and refortified. Fort Slocum was established to supplement the defenses on nearby Davids' Island in the western end of Long Island Sound in the city of New Rochelle, New York.

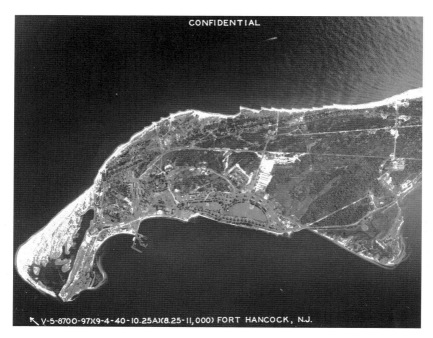

Fort Hancock.

Fort Hamilton.

Fort Totten.

Fort Jay.

Fort Wadsworth.

Fort Slocum.

DEVELOPING BETTER STICKS AND STONES

I know not with what weapons World War III will be fought, but World War IV will be fought with sticks and stones.

—Albert Einstein

Let's step back a few decades before the construction of these forts and batteries were completed. These early modernization concepts were tasked to the U.S. Army Corps of Engineers, which would build the new batteries, and Ordnance Corps, which started designing more substantial and powerful guns and ammunition. All of these, of course, had to be tested before being constructed en masse and entrusted with protecting our coasts.

The new designs for weaponry had rendered obsolete the old smoothbore guns and cannonballs used during the Civil War and replaced them with a sizeable missile-like projectile, conically shaped with a pointed nose that could be fired like a rocket from the muzzle of a cannon. This technological innovation, called heavy rifled ordnance, would be applied to all weapons going forward.

Rifling is the term for the circular grooves cut into the inside of a steel gun barrel that impart a spin on the projectile as it travels through the barrel. Much like the throw of a football by a quarterback with a perfect spiral, this spinning motion stabilizes the projectile in flight, giving it a faster speed, greater accuracy and a much longer range. It was the use of heavy rifled ordnance during the Union bombardment of the Confederate Fort Pulaski in Georgia in 1862 that was the death knell of old stone forts. Fort Pulaski, made of brick, was reduced to rubble, and its walls collapsed from a twenty-four-hour attack with the modern rifled guns firing the newer projectiles.

By 1872, President Ulysses S. Grant had approved funding for the experimentation and testing of heavy rifled ordnance. The Secretary of War then convened a board to review some forty proposals from inventors for the manufacture of breech-loading as well as muzzle-loading guns.

Interestingly, what the United States was proposing to do was already being done in some of the European countries, so we were a bit behind the curve. As a result, the Secretary of War started looking for locations for a "proving and experimental ground," as he described it.

They needed a testing range of at least six miles with level ground and close to a railroad line. And it had to be on land that was currently owned by the government or inexpensive to purchase.

Left: Cannon balls. *Right*: Artillery shell.

Several potential sites for the proving ground were considered within New Jersey as well as Long Island. Most of the sites, however, had too many people moving into the area, as the 1870s saw the Jersey Shore swell because it was fast becoming America's premier tourist destination. The government, however, did own a reservation on Sandy Hook, which was about eighteen miles from New York City as the crow flies. It was the ideal location for a proving ground and was selected for use by the War Department and the army.

Standing at the very tip of Sandy Hook, you could see the waterfront of Brooklyn and Staten Island, with New York City beyond. As the seagull flies, Sandy Hook is about eight miles across the water from New York. Today, the large passenger ships and freighters entering Sandy Hook and Raritan Bay slide right past the tip of Sandy Hook very carefully, using the natural deep-water channel that has guided mariners into these waters since the 1600s. It's an odd sight, one which never ceases to amaze me—how can they come so close without crashing onto the shoreline?

Sandy Hook, comprising 1,665 acres, has one of the largest colonies of nesting shorebirds in New Jersey, and its holly forest is one of the largest on the East Coast. Also, about 70 percent of the plants growing on Sandy Hook are poison ivy. And oddly, without poison ivy, Sandy Hook could have been a shallow sandbar. Instead, the extensive root system of poison ivy actually traps wind-blown sand and has allowed the area to build itself up so other plants could grow.

Today, tens of thousands of tourists come to Sandy Hook every summer to hike, swim, explore, bird watch and ride bicycles. There's even a clothing-optional beach if that's your thing. And, of course, lots of people enjoy visiting the Sandy Hook Lighthouse. Built in 1764, it is the oldest standing and operating lighthouse in the United States. But not everyone has the complete knowledge of what happened here in the story of the defense of our country. Tourists can see some of the remains of an extensive military installation that protected New York as they view dozens of uniformly designed buildings and ancient gun batteries. I'm pretty confident not everyone knows what occurred here. Most people are amazed when they learn just how vital this sleepy little peninsula was in protecting our nation.

Whenever exploring Sandy Hook, I continually discover things half-buried in the sand or revealed within a grove of holly bushes in a wooded area. Fortunately, for me, I was given the "cook's tour" of Sandy Hook while working on an eight-hour documentary on its history. I saw and learned things about Sandy Hook's past that blew me away, such as artillery batteries and even underground missile launch sites.

Everything I saw was eventually made obsolete by technological advances. And although no shots were ever fired in battle, thunder rumbled across Sandy Hook for decades as new weapons were tested on its beaches and the massive gun batteries held target practice.

In 1874, the very first test was undertaken at the Sandy Hook Proving Ground to fire a 10-inch gun loaded with 35 pounds of gunpowder packed behind a 170-pound shell or projectile. This was a unique test because it was a smoothbore gun that had been converted to an 8-inch gun with a rifled sleeve fitted in its barrel.

The men involved in this first test took cover in a bombproof vault some twenty feet from the gun, which was fired and tested for two days.

The Proof Battery where new weapons were tested.

One of the largest guns ever tested at Sandy Hook.

About seven hundred rounds or firings were completed. And after each firing, the gun's bore, or the inside of the barrel, was examined for damage or erosion. Rifled barrels wear out faster than smoothbore ones because there is more surface area that receives friction, and the iron or steel is slowly ground away one round at a time. Smoothbore guns have a more considerable tolerance and generally don't experience the same issues. Barrels on guns were eventually replaced because the army wanted gun barrels that would last longer. So after two days of testing, the notes from the person who did the initial testing read: "This gun is sound and serviceable." In other words, the tests were successful, and the proving ground was up and running.

Congress was pleased with the results, and it was determined that a more massive thirty-five-ton gun would also be tested. In those days, big was always considered better. Great Britain had recently built an eighty-one-ton weapon, so the United States followed suit and started testing bigger guns. As warships grew in size with the Industrial Revolution, the cannons that would be needed to fight them grew as well.

It was determined during these tests that newer and better weapons had to be developed to destroy the new ironclad vessels, which were being used toward the end of the Civil War and were now appearing in some European countries. It was also becoming apparent that not only guns and barrels needed testing but also carriages in which they sat when fired.

Activity at the Sandy Hook Proving Ground was hot and heavy as it tested hundreds of various types of weapons beginning in 1875. And a lot of private scientists and manufacturers were starting to participate in the development and testing of new weaponry. They were actually competing with one another, with the end result being the most efficient and practical designs available. Soon all kinds of guns—small and large—were being tested, like pistols and rifles as well as machine guns.

In 1875, the Secretary of the Treasury asked the Secretary of War to develop a line-throwing gun that could shoot a rope from the beach to a stranded vessel during heavy storms. This would facilitate the use of a block and tackle that would ferry the survivors safely to the shore. So it wasn't always about war; this was for humanitarian reasons. The Proving Ground was conveniently located next to both the Sandy Hook and Spermaceti Cove Life-Saving Stations (which we discussed earlier), so they agreed to develop and test a gun that could fire a lifeline to ships in trouble. The Lyle gun, as it came to be known, went on to save thousands of lives from stranded ships and was used until the 1960s, when it was finally superseded by the helicopter as the primary means of shipwreck rescue.

Meanwhile, the Ordnance Department began hiring civilian mechanics in 1879; they were paid as much as $2.75 a day.

Testing weapons at the Sandy Hook Proving Ground. *From* Harper's Weekly, *1871.*

A lot of the guns being tested in those days were very heavy—like tens of tons—so a so-called sling wagon was brought to help move and mount the guns for testing. During the 1870s, supplies and gun parts and barrels were being shipped to Sandy Hook regularly. The wharf, or pier, which had been built in the late 1850s by the U.S. Army Corps of Engineers, was upgraded to handle all the shipments.

In 1876, a steam launch or boat was transferred to the Ordnance Department to facilitate transportation of government officials from New York City to Sandy Hook so they could view the tests or attend meetings and meet with the manufacturers.

By 1885, the next president, Grover Cleveland, had formed a special board chaired by his Secretary of War, William Endicott, to review and make recommendations for our national defense based on the weapons being developed and tested by the ordnance department.

The board proposed an enormous number of armored turrets and casemates to be armed with "weapons of unprecedented size and firepower." They had also recommended establishing modern fortifications at twenty-six coastal locations and harbors, including Sandy Hook. Some were existing army posts, while others would be built from scratch.

The Sandy Hook Mortar Battery, built in 1890, was among the first two concrete gun batteries built on Sandy Hook that were part of the modern

Mortars on Sandy Hook (1915).

New York Harbor defenses against attack from the sea. The use of concrete was nearly unprecedented and would have amazing long-term effects in not only military engineering but in civilian architecture as well. Lift-Gun Battery Number 1, also built of concrete and equipped with a state-of-the-art hydraulic elevator system that would lift massive twelve-inch caliber guns to its roof so they could fire, was also built nearby at the same time.

Meanwhile, at the adjacent Sandy Hook Proving Ground, the guns being tested would occasionally malfunction and even explode, such as a ten-inch gun being tested using 35-pound powder charges and 181-pound projectiles. As the 312th round was fired, the gun burst into fragments that hurtled hundreds of yards. Two men were killed and three injured when the ten-inch shell exploded. These were the first fatalities at the Proving Ground. Sadly, they wouldn't be the last.

Unfortunately, in 1895, another fatality occurred at the proof battery. This time, a four-and-a-half-inch rifle burst apart, killing young First Lieutenant Fremont Peck of the Ordnance Corps and wounding a nearby sergeant. One year later, another gun exploded, killing two soldiers and injuring four.

Three years later, the United States became concerned about the possibility of a war with Spain. Following the explosion of the USS *Maine*, an American battleship in the harbor of Havana, Cuba, the defense of New York Harbor against attack became a top concern for the country. We finally declared war against Spain in 1898. A massive building program occurred at Fort Hancock as the East Coast braced for an attack. It was a short war, however, and no Spanish ships ever threatened New York or New Jersey. As a result of an American victory in the war, we gained Guam and the Philippines in the Pacific, as well as Puerto Rico and Cuba in the Caribbean.

By 1901, the Proving Ground had almost ninety enlisted men stationed there. The size and scope of the operations there were increasing by leaps and bounds as the cannons and gun carriages grew in size and scale.

With a new concrete firing line and test facility installed in 1906, a gun park, as it was called, was built. This is where equipment, barrels and projectiles would be stored before testing. The area also had many concrete skids with iron rails, so the sling wagon could move quickly from the gun park to the gun battery with guns and equipment to be tested.

A new seventy-thousand-pound locomotive was purchased along with several passenger cars to carry civilian technicians and employees to and from where they lived. On an average day, the train carried 180 passengers. During the year, the train also carried some fourteen million pounds of equipment.

For nearly a decade, the proving ground tested every new weapon, explosive powder, fuses, gun carriages and the like. You name it, it came to the Sandy Hook Proving Ground. If it could be fired, it would be tested, and if it passed all of the tests, it would be manufactured and then tested again before anything was put in the hands of our soldiers.

By 1919, testing larger and larger guns proved to be too dangerous for either civilian ships at sea or for Sea Bright, New Jersey, which was now a stone's throw away from where the shells from more powerful guns started landing. As a result, the entire facility was relocated to Aberdeen, Maryland, where it operates today as a functional proving ground to develop and test new weapons.

14

THE IMMIGRANTS

FROM WHERE DID EVERYBODY COME?

Give me your tired, your poor, your huddled masses yearning to breathe free, the wretched refuse of your teeming shore. Send these, the homeless, tempest-tossed to me. I lift my lamp beside the golden door.

—*Emma Lazarus*

Somebody counted 327 million American citizens in 2018. The population is expected to hit 355 million by 2030, 373 million by 2040 and 388 million by 2050.

Between 1892 and 1954, we counted more than twelve million immigrants entering the United States through Ellis Island. I guess we're growing.

In case you don't know, Ellis Island is in New York Harbor near the Statue of Liberty. The island was initially a little more than three acres. What many people don't know about the island is it was increased to more than twenty-seven acres using the landfill from the ballasts of ships and extra dirt left over during construction of the New York City subway system.

Before the island became the so-called Gateway to America, local Indian tribes called it Kioshk, or Gull Island, after the birds that were once its only inhabitants. It was also known as Oyster Island during the Dutch and English colonial periods because of the great abundance of oyster beds surrounding it.

Immigrants arriving at Ellis Island in 1902. *National Geographic*.

In the 1770s, Samuel Ellis purchased the island, and before long, it was transformed into a hangout for pirates.

By 1790, the population of the United States was fast approaching four million people. Ten years later, more than five million people were living here.

By 1808, the federal government had purchased Ellis Island from New York State and built Fort Gibson and installed guns to defend New York Harbor. As we previously discussed, Fort Gibson was part of a defensive system that included forts throughout the area, such as Castle Williams on Governor's Island, Fort Wood on Bedloe's Island and two primitive forts at the entrance to New York Harbor by the Verrazano Narrows.

In 1824, the first dry dock in America was completed on the East River, where the location and depth were perfect for larger ships. By the time the Erie Canal was completed in 1825, New York had become the nation's most important shipping port.

By 1840, more passengers and a greater tonnage of cargo had arrived through the port of New York than all of the other principal harbors in the country combined. In 1870, New York City began seriously developing its waterfront. By 1900, it was one of the greatest and busiest ports in the entire world.

By the turn of the twentieth century, railroad terminals lined the western banks of the North River (today's Hudson River) in Hudson County to transport passengers as well as freight from all over the United States.

The freight was ferried across the river by the competing railroads with small fleets of towboats, barges and 323 car floats, which were specially designed barges with rails so railroad cars could be rolled onto the barge. New York subsidized this service to undercut competitive ports.

The Statue of Liberty (*Liberty Enlightening the World*) was dedicated in 1886 and designated as a National Monument in 1924. Today, it stands on Liberty Island in the harbor as a symbol of the period when so many came to the United States at the turn of the twentieth century.

By 1890, there were sixty-three million people in our country. In 1892, Ellis Island became the entrance for the first massive wave of immigrants coming from countries like England, Ireland, Germany and the Scandinavian countries. These and other countries in Europe were experiencing political instability, restrictive religious laws and horrible economic conditions, which stimulated the largest migration of people in the history of the world through the 1800s and the later 1900s.

The first official immigrant to America, arriving on January 1, 1892, was Annie Moore. She was an Irish teenage girl. Behind her were twelve million more immigrants who would be processed for the next sixty-two years.

Annie, along with her two younger brothers, was on a boat anchored off the southern tip of Manhattan. She had left Ireland on a steamship to start her new life in America. She spent twelve days aboard the ship dreaming about reuniting with her family after being apart from them for four years.

Annie Moore passed through Ellis Island and lived her entire life within a few square blocks on Manhattan's Lower East Side. She died from heart failure at the age of fifty in 1924.

The immigration station she had walked through to enter her new life in America burned to the ground in 1897, along with the registry books listing every immigrant who had landed in New York City since 1855, including the name of Annie Moore.

Today, a statue of Annie Moore and her brothers exists on Ellis Island.

During the early 1900s, 76,212,168 people listed the United States as their residence. We thought the wave of immigration had reached its crest, but we were wrong.

By the early 1900s, it took under five days to cross the Atlantic Ocean from England to America.

MAKING MONEY IN THE MILLIONS

This land may be profitable to those that will adventure it.
                                                    —*Henry Hudson*

As you might expect, many immigrants coming to America had dreams of being successful in life and business. It was a time when entrepreneurs could get rich. Many did get rich, and some got even richer.

Before the American Revolution, each colony had a distinct financial currency, but each adhered to the pound, shilling and pence denominations. The prevalence of the Spanish dollar in the colonies led to the money of the United States being denominated in dollars rather than pounds. One by one, colonies began to issue their own paper money to serve as a convenient medium of exchange.

The word *millionaire* was first used to describe the wealth made by John Law (1671–1729), a Scottish economist who believed that money was only a means of exchange that did not constitute wealth in itself and that national wealth depended on trade. Law was also a gambler, and he became head of French finances on the speculation that his company had exclusive trading rights in Louisiana, and this would create enormous profits. John Law gave the name *New Orleans* to the large city at the mouth of the Mississippi River to honor one of his backers at court. His fortune was counted in French francs, however, and not in American dollars.

The first American millionaire in America, however, was Elias Hasket Derby (1739–1799), a sea merchant who began trading with China.

Here are some other immigrants who became millionaires in America:

John Jacob Astor Sr. (1763–1848) was born in Germany and began as a fur trader. In 1783, he came to America and started developing real estate, which led to helping build modern New York City. In 1816, he began smuggling opium from China but stopped after a few years.

John McDonogh (1779–1850) was born in Baltimore, Maryland, and became a southern landholder and slave owner.

Cornelius Vanderbilt (1794–1877) was born on Staten Island, New York, and became an American business magnate who built his wealth in railroads and shipping. After working in his father's business, Vanderbilt worked his way into leadership positions in the domestic water trade and invested heavily in the rapidly growing railroad industry.

Meyer Guggenheim (1828–1905) was born in Switzerland and eventually arrived in America during 1847. Over the next few decades, the family became known for their worldwide successes in mining and smelting, including the American Smelting and Refining Company. Eventually, the family possessed one of the largest fortunes in the world.

An interesting story about the Guggenheim family is when it was shipping 7,678 bars of silver on a trip across Raritan Bay near the mouth of the Arthur Kill in 1903. Unfortunately, the barge capsized, and the cargo of silver ingots slipped into the murky Raritan Bay. Salvage efforts to retrieve the silver resulted in recovering 6,000 bars of silver, but 1,678 were still at the bottom of the bay. If found today, they'd be worth more than $30 million. The *New York Times* printed a story about the missing silver ingots, and treasure hunters rushed to the bay to search for them. As far as anyone knows, they've never been found.

Jay Gould (1836–1892) was born in Roxbury, New York, and, like Vanderbilt, made his fortune in the railroads.

Andrew Carnegie (1835–1919) was born in Scotland and became known in America as both an industrialist and philanthropist.

John D. Rockefeller (1839–1937) was an oil magnate and real estate developer.

Henry Ford (1863–1947) invented and popularized the automobile.

Robert Wood Johnson Jr. (1893–1968) was chairman of Johnson & Johnson, a company founded by his father.

J. Paul Getty (1892–1976) was an oil tycoon.

Today, about 6 percent of the population (more than seven million households) in the United States are millionaires.

15

THE ENEMIES

GERMANY'S SECRET PLAN TO INVADE AMERICA

Germany must have her place in the sun.

—*Kaiser Wilhelm II*

While America thrived in the times of prosperity at the turn of the century, Imperial Germany was developing plans for the invasion of the United States. The plans, ordered by Germany's Kaiser Wilhelm II, were developed between 1897 and 1903. He intended not to conquer our nation but to reduce our country's influence in the rest of the world. As always, the existence of America's freedoms and industrial might posed the greatest threat to tyrants. Kaiser Wilhelm was no exception

We didn't know it at the time, but his invasion was supposed to force the United States to bargain from a weakened position. Furthermore, the invasion would sever America's growing economic and political connections in the Pacific Ocean, the Caribbean and South America so that Germany's influence could be increased in those parts of the world.

Here's the spoiler alert: His junior officers provided the Kaiser with several proposals, but none was seriously considered. By 1906, the secret plans had turned to dust and faded away. The plans didn't become public until they were discovered in the German military archive in 1970.

Kaiser Wilhelm II (1902).

TENSIONS GROW WITH GERMANY

War! What is it good for? Absolutely nothing!
—Barrett Strong and Norman Whitfield, lyrics of "War"

In 1901, coastal artillery units were created by re-designating the heavy artillery companies that previously garrisoned harbor forts, and by 1907, the United States Army Coast Artillery Corps had been established as an official branch of service to operate the country's new coast defenses.

Due to the development of dreadnought battleships in Europe, a new fourteen-inch gun was introduced. Improved models of other weapons were also introduced. By the beginning of World War I, the United States had a coastal defense system that was equal to any other country

While America had a state-of-the-art coast artillery defense system, the early 1900s and World War I introduced a new weapon of war—the airplane.

Inside the National Air and Space Museum in Washington, D.C., the original 1903 and 1909 Wright Flyer, the world's first military airplane, is on display. After their design was brought to a level of practicality in 1905, the

Wright brothers looked for a customer for their invention. An obvious choice was the U.S. Army, which had already been developing an aeronautical program with lighter-than-air vehicles, such as balloons. In fact, observation balloons had been in use since the Civil War.

The U.S. Army Signal Corps called for bids for a two-seat observation aircraft in 1908, and so Orville Wright came to Fort Myer, Virginia, with an airplane to meet the army's performance requirements. Midway through the trials, on September 17, 1908, the Wright airplane malfunctioned and crashed, severely injuring Orville and killing his passenger, Lieutenant Thomas Selfridge, the army's official observer.

Both Wilbur and Orville returned to Fort Myer in 1909 with a new airplane and successfully completed the trials. The Signal Corps officially accepted the Wright airplane, the first one purchased and put into service by any government.

Attacks from above the oceans and harbors weren't the only potential threats to America that emerged during this time—they came from below the water's surface as well. Submarine designs began to flourish in many nations during this period. In the United States, the USS *Holland* became the navy's first modern commissioned submarine designed for military use. Designed by John Holland, it was built at the Crescent Shipyard of Elizabeth, New Jersey, and launched in 1897.

Unfortunately, there was some competition among the inventors of the first military submarine. There was even a little competition in the claim of who was first. One person who claimed to be the first was Simon Lake.

America's first military submarine after the Civil War.

SUBMERGING SIMON'S SUBMARINE

I must confess that my imagination refuses to see any sort of submarine doing anything but suffocating its crew and floundering at sea.

—*H.G. Wells*

When visiting Atlantic Highlands, New Jersey, today, you might see what looks like a giant wooden watermelon. It's actually a replica of one of the first submarines designed and built by Simon Lake, an inventor and entrepreneur, who lived in the Jersey Bayshore area with his aunt and uncle. Across the Shrewsbury River from the smoke and thunder of the tests at the Sandy Hook Proving Ground, the future of submarine design took shape. Many historians credit him with developing the technology that led to the production of modern submarines.

Eventually, his company built thirty-three submarines for the U.S. Navy between 1909 and 1922. During his lifetime, Lake registered more than two hundred patents on such innovations as marine salvage, shipbuilding, Arctic exploration and prefabricated housing.

Simon Lake was born in 1866 and went to school in Toms River, New Jersey. Actually, most of his family members were prolific inventors. For example, his father invented the roller window shade, and his grandfather played a crucial role in developing the seaside resorts of Ocean City and

Simon Lake's *Defender*, built in 1907.

Atlantic City. His uncle conceived the basic idea for the Caterpillar™ tractor while building an access road to Atlantic City from the mainland.

After reading *Twenty Thousand Leagues Under the Sea* by Jules Verne, young Simon Lake was intrigued with undersea travel and exploration. When the U.S. Navy offered a public contest in 1893 to design a submarine, he quickly decided to enter it. Lake and seven other inventors submitted designs hoping to win the competition. Unfortunately, he didn't win but gained some degree of notoriety.

Undeterred by his loss in the contest, Lake was determined to build submarines, so a year later, he made a crude wooden submarine he called *Argonaut Junior*. Others referred to it as the "pitch-pine submarine." It was nothing more than a large wooden box that could sink to the bottom and crawl forward on a set of man-powered wheels. A compressed tank of air was used both to "blow" the ballast tanks for returning to the surface and to pressurize the interior to keep water out when a trapdoor was opened in the floor to give access to the bottom of a bay or river or ocean.

Lake's first demonstration of *Argonaut Junior* was in 1894 off a pier in Atlantic Highlands at the mouth of the Navesink River in location called Black Hole, across from Black Point (today's Rumson). Actually, it was the same location where Patriot Joshua Huddy escaped from the British by jumping from a boat and swimming ashore during the Revolution.

As a result of his success in demonstrating his submarine, Lake was able to attract enough investors to start the Lake Submarine Company and to design and manufacture submarines within a year.

Then in 1898, he took his first manufactured submarine into the Atlantic Ocean for a test dive. His first dive was off Cape Henry in Virginia. His next excursion underwater was from Norfolk, Virginia, to Sandy Hook, New Jersey. Lake mostly traveled on the surface but would regularly submerge to explore shipwrecks as he went along. His journey to Sandy Hook was the first substantial voyage by a submersible craft in the ocean. As a result of his successful test, Lake received a telegram of congratulations from Jules Verne.

During Lake's career, he was credited with a vast number of achievements in the development of submarines used by both the military and for marine salvaging. As a result, Simon Lake is considered to be the "Father of Modern Submarines."

As previously mentioned, however, it was John Holland who was the first to sell his idea to the U.S. Navy.

PREPARING FOR WORLD WAR I

Submarines and airplanes became more critically important, with the former being a perceived, if not actual, threat to U.S. harbors. This concern caused an increase in the use of mines and nets and increased demand for superior coastal artillery. As World War I raged in Europe from 1914 to 1917, neutral America remained determined to stay isolated from the killing grounds. Hunkered down behind its coastal batteries, the United States sent humanitarian aid and watched from afar but refused to become involved in combat.

While submarines posed no serious threat to the harbors themselves, German submarines wreaked havoc in the Atlantic Ocean. The sinking of neutral American ships by these submarines would ultimately pull the United States into the war.

Curiously, despite the rise of airpower during this era, it received little consideration in our coastal defenses until the late 1920s, after tests revealed warships could be sunk by aerial bombing.

Later, our lines of defense also utilized explosive underwater mines placed at the entrance to New York Harbor that provided enhanced protection from both submarines and ships. We also had large nets fixed underwater to prevent enemy submarines from entering the harbor.

Due to their experience and training with large guns, the coastal artillery units were sent overseas with the American Expeditionary Force in 1917 and operated massive "siege" artillery and railroad guns, primarily French- and British-made weapons.

The First World War began in 1914, but as mentioned, the United States kept its distance for as long as possible.

Some historians say the war was the result of the assassination of the Austrian archduke Franz Ferdinand and his wife by a Bosnian revolutionary. Other historians disagree and say it was far more complicated.

Many alliances were signed between European countries from 1879 to 1914. These were important because they meant that some countries had to declare war if one of their allies declared war first. If that wasn't binding enough, many of the monarchs of the day were all related to one another.

The dawn of the twentieth century found the Old World at a crossroads. Spain had been knocked from its pedestal by the United States, which emerged on the world stage as a viable force. And remember our friends, the British, and their empire, which they tried to include us in but failed?

By 1900, the British Empire comprised more than five continents. France controlled large parts of Africa, as did Belgium. The lands "owned" by Britain, France and other European nations made the Germans jealous because they wanted to expand their existing colonies and acquire new ones just like all the other key players.

This competition among countries to build empires led to an arms race between all of the largest countries. Both France and Germany more than doubled the number of their troops between 1870 and 1914, and there was fierce competition between Britain and Germany for mastery of the oceans.

As previously mentioned, the British had introduced the Dreadnought battleship to the world in 1906. This all-modern steel warship made every other warship in the world obsolete in an instant. Not to be outdone, Germany introduced its own deadly battleships. In fact, it was the battleship construction program of the world's navies that constituted the first real global arms race. From the early 1900s to 1914, these monster ships—and their massive guns—grew by size and number. With Germany and England staring at each other across the North Sea, the swelling numbers of warships only fueled the tensions between the nations.

Von Schlieffen, a German military official, also drew up a plan of action to attack France through Belgium when Russia attacked Germany. Thank goodness we weren't involved in this mishmash of intentions. When World War I finally erupted in 1914, it was the world's first taste of the concept of mutually assured destruction, as each country declared war on each other. America looked on in horror but would not join in. Not yet, anyway.

In the meantime, the American public was becoming increasingly more negative toward Germany than toward any other country in Europe. After all, Germany and Kaiser Wilhelm were the primary aggressors.

Then, on May 1, 1915, the largest passenger ship in the world—RMS *Lusitania*—left New York Harbor and entered Raritan Bay on its last voyage from New York City. Six days later, the *Lusitania* was torpedoed by a German U-boat off the coast of Ireland, killing more than 1,000 people, including 114 Americans. American citizens were enraged at the sinking, which was considered to be a barbaric war crime.

During these days, President Woodrow Wilson made virtually all the critical decisions regarding America's foreign policy. While our country was at peace, American financial institutions made significant loans to France and Britain so they could buy munitions, needed materials and even food from countries on the western side of the Atlantic Ocean.

Unfortunately, before 1917, President Wilson had made minimal preparation for a war on land. We did, however, expand the navy to prepare for any future battles at sea.

By 1917, Russia had begun experiencing political turmoil. Great Britain and France were having economic difficulties. Germany experienced military successes in the trenches on the western front while its ally, the Ottoman Empire, held on to territory in what is today Iraq, Israel and Syria.

Germany, sensing its power starting to grow, resumed unrestricted submarine warfare against Britain's freighters in an attempt to starve England and thereby force it to surrender. Simultaneously, the German High Command warned that sinking any ships flying American flags would probably force America into the war.

Our resolve to lend a hand and enter the war came serendipitously when British intelligence advised us that an encoded message, known as the Zimmermann Telegram, was sent from Germany to Mexico. The message was a secret offer to help Mexico regain territories it lost during the Mexican-American War if it would become an ally of Germany and invade the southern United States. That's when President Wilson asked Congress for "a war to end all wars" that would "make the world safe for democracy." Congress voted to declare war on Germany on April 6, 1917.

U.S. troops began arriving on the western front in large numbers during the summer of 1917, and tens of thousands followed into 1918. America was now fighting its first global war, and American soldiers were fighting on European soil for the very first time.

The amount of work being done at the Sandy Hook Proving Ground multiplied while immigration into the United States dramatically decreased for the first time. There was so much demand for new weaponry during this period that the Proving Ground had to be moved to Aberdeen, Maryland, just to meet the needs of the war.

However, Fort Hancock and Sandy Hook still had a vital role to play. The Sandy Hook Ordnance Depot was established at the southern end of the peninsula in 1917. This massive installation was constructed to store all of the ammunition being earmarked for use by the American troops for significant offensive operations being scheduled for 1918 and 1919.

Meanwhile, during the war, the United States continually surveyed the horizon of the Atlantic Ocean. We knew German submarines, or U-boats, were patrolling our coast and annihilating Allied merchant ships. However, they were difficult to find through a telescope if they remained submerged.

German U-boat.

One German submarine sank the USS *San Diego*, a U.S. Navy light cruiser, just off the coast of Long Island, New York, in 1918. Unfortunately, our limited number of planes during the time patrolled American waters only during the day, leaving the U-boats to operate offshore and in adverse weather or at night.

The U-boats continually tried to disrupt Allied maritime operations in the Atlantic Ocean off the New Jersey coast by laying mines. In all, they would sink thirteen Allied merchant vessels off the coast and claim many lives during the war.

A steel net was sunk across the Verrazano Narrows between Brooklyn and Staten Island to keep German submarines out of the inner harbor. Believe it or not, German submarines put floating mines around Sandy Hook, so we turned sixteen of our tugboats into minesweepers. They would look for mines every day, sweeping as far out from Sandy Hook as one hundred miles.

One of our harbor pilot boats got tangled in the submarine net and was accidentally rammed and sunk by a larger ship. Pilot boats were used to transport maritime pilots between land and the inbound or outbound ships that they were piloting. These harbor pilots, who have served New York Harbor since the 1600s, were experienced seamen and had expert knowledge of the harbor, which they used to safely bring ships in and out of the channels.

DISASTER ON AND NEAR THE RARITAN RIVER

The Raritan Arsenal was established in 1918 on the north bank of the Raritan River near the present-day town of Edison, New Jersey. Its purpose was to provide a storage and shipping terminal for military supplies, equipment and munitions headed overseas.

After the First World War, it then became a permanent ordnance depot where army vehicles could be stored and ammunition could be received, stored and shipped, such as 37mm and 40mm projectiles, grenades and dynamite. From 1919 to 1941, a training facility was located here. Unfortunately, during this same period, several accidental explosions occurred in buildings and outdoor areas where explosives were stored. The T.A. Gillespie Company Shell Loading Plant—sometimes called the Morgan Munitions Depot—exploded in 1918 in the Morgan area of Sayreville in Middlesex County, New Jersey.

The initial explosion, which many believe may have been caused by a cigarette, set off a series of explosions and fires that burned for three days. The full force of the blast was estimated to be six kilotons. It literally vaporized more than one hundred people and injured many hundreds more.

This facility loaded large artillery shells with high explosives for use during World War I and was one of the largest plants of its type in the world. Not only was the facility wholly destroyed, but so were more than three hundred other buildings in the vicinity as well. As a result, the town of Sayreville and neighboring South Amboy had to be evacuated. For more than a century after the event, debris from the explosion would regularly be found in a radius of more than a mile.

Damages from the explosion were some $18 million. According to military experts at the time, the explosion resulted in delaying ammunition to supply the western front for six months. Luckily, the war ended one month after the explosion. The explosion went down in history as one of the most massive man-made nonnuclear explosions of all time. Some of the strongest blasts from exploding storehouses broke windows as far away as New York City and Asbury Park—both some twenty miles away.

Nearly a century later, unexploded ordnance from the facility was still being found in the surrounding area. For example, in 2007, ordnance was discovered at an elementary school while workers were grading an area for a playground.

Eleven years after the blast, the South Amboy Lions Club erected a monument at the site of a twenty-by-thirty-five-foot mass grave for those lost

Crater from explosion at the shell plant in Morgan, New Jersey.

in the blast. The inscription reads: "In memory of the unidentified dead who gave their lives while in the service of the United States of America, at the Morgan Shell Loading Plant in the explosion of October 4–5, 1918." You can visit the grave and memorial near the entrance of the Ernst Memorial Cemetery at 328 Ernston Road in Parlin, New Jersey.

World War I, which lasted from 1914 to 1918, finally shuddered to a halt after claiming at least twelve million lives. The world would never be the same. Germany formally surrendered on November 11, 1918, and all nations agreed to stop fighting while the terms of peace were negotiated. On June 28, 1919, Germany and the Allied Nations (Britain, France, Italy and Russia) signed the Treaty of Versailles, formally ending the war.

A SHARK IN THE CREEK

Ok, ok, you're gonna need a bigger boat!
—*Chief Brody in the movie* JAWS

So while we were right in the middle of fighting Germany in World War I, several shark attacks along the Jersey Shore and a creek in Matawan and Keyport, New Jersey, had our citizens in this area spooked.

The Jersey Shore shark attacks of July 1916 were a series of incidents along the coast of New Jersey that killed four people and injured one. Unfortunately, it was a scorching summer, so thousands of people were frolicking in the surf at the Jersey Shore and wading in the water along Raritan Bay.

The first shark attack occurred at Beach Haven, which was a resort town on Long Beach Island off the southern coast of New Jersey. A twenty-five-year-old man was on vacation with his family. Before dinner, he decided to swim in the Atlantic Ocean as a dog was playing on the beach. Shortly after entering the water, the man began shouting, and many people thought he was calling to the dog. Instead, a shark was attacking his leg. Fortunately, a lifeguard rescued him by pulling the man to shore. A bystander reported that the shark followed as they pulled the bleeding man from the water. Unfortunately, he bled to death on the manager's desk of a seaside hotel.

Despite the attack, the beaches along the Jersey Shore stayed open. Ship captains even reported seeing sharks swarming off the coast of New Jersey, but the beaches remained accessible.

Then came a second attack forty-five miles north of the first attack in Spring Lake. The victim was a twenty-seven-year-old man who was a bell captain at one of the hotels. He was swimming 130 yards from the shore when a shark bit him in the abdomen and then severed his legs. The water turned red as people on the beach screamed. Two lifeguards rowed out to the victim and pulled him from the water, but he bled to death on the way to shore.

The next two significant attacks took place in the freshwater Matawan Creek near the towns of Keyport and Matawan, some thirty miles northwest of Spring Lake and inland of Raritan Bay. While a local sea captain and resident of Matawan witnessed an eight-foot shark in Matawan Creek swimming upstream, the town dismissed his report.

Meanwhile, a group of local boys decided to go skinny-dipping upstream from where someone had spotted the shark. They were swimming near Wyckoff Dock, where steamships would arrive to visit Matawan.

While swimming on a sweltering day, they saw what appeared to be an "old, black weather-beaten board or a weathered log." In reality, it was the dorsal fin of the shark, but the young boys didn't know it yet. Finally, they could see what it was and began to move quickly out of the water. Unfortunately, one boy was pulled underwater by the shark.

The terrified boys ran into town for help, and several people came to the creek to investigate. Some of the men dived into the water, which was now colored red from blood. They eventually found the young boy's body. While trying to pull the boy's lifeless body to shore, one of the men was also bitten by the shark. People from the town were now gathering on the shore and gasped in horror when they witnessed the attack.

Local townspeople search for body of victim.

Unfortunately, the young boy had died, but the twenty-four-year-old man who tried to rescue the boy was still alive. Unfortunately, however, he was losing lots of blood. He was rushed to Monmouth Memorial Hospital in Long Branch but bled to death before anyone could help him.

The fifth and final victim was fourteen years old. He was visiting a relative and swimming in the creek in Keyport that same day and about a mile from the attack in Matawan. The shark bit his left leg, but his brother and friend rescued him after a vicious tug-of-war battle with the shark. He was taken to a hospital and recovered.

Remember that people living before 1916 didn't know much about sharks, so the attacks were beginning to shape the public perception of what sharks were all about.

Following the incredible attack in a freshwater creek, a national wave of panic followed. Fishing boats led the population to hunt and kill sharks so that the economic spiral downward would be nipped in the bud. Many towns along the Jersey Shore and Raritan Bay began enclosing the public beaches with steel nets to protect swimmers. Rewards were announced for anyone who could catch the shark that was killing people. Many people claimed they caught the shark, and one person actually cut open a shark to show human remains, but it proved to be a hoax.

The *New York Times*, like many newspapers, featured a headline that read, "Shark Kills Bather Off Jersey Beach." Newspaper accounts such as these cost coastal communities tourist trade for the remainder of the summer. Even sunbathing experienced a considerable decline. After all, who knew if sharks could climb out of the water and onto the beaches to attack sunbathers?

The public reaction or overreaction led to a press conference at the American Museum of Natural History with scientists whose intent was to calm the public panic by educating folks about sharks.

Following the attacks, sharks were seen more frequently than ever before. Maybe it was because more people were looking for them. Hundreds of sharks were captured and killed as this search for sharks became the largest animal hunt in history. No further attacks were reported along the Jersey Shore for the rest of 1916. And it was never proven whether it was one or several sharks, what species or if it was ever caught.

Bull sharks have been known to survive and even thrive in fresh water. For example, sharks live in a freshwater lake in South America. There was a bounty offered for dead freshwater sharks because they had killed and severely injured bathers in the lake in 1944.

LAND SHARKS

Loose lips sink ships.
—American propaganda campaign (World War II)

You'd think that with the First World War now over, we'd be able to rest a bit. However, between 1918 and 1919, suspected enemy agents were detained while regular inspection of arriving immigrants was conducted aboard ship or at the docks.

By the end of World War I, a big Red Scare of communism spread across America, and thousands of suspected alien radicals were stopped at the Immigration Depot on Ellis Island. Hundreds were deported.

By 1920, the population exceeded 100 million people. By 1921, the Quota Laws had been passed, and in 1924, the National Origins Act was enacted. Both of these laws restricted the number of ethnic groups entering the country based on the number already living in the United States.

Incidentally, Ellis Island and the Statue of Liberty were both declared a National Monument in 1965. Five years later, the population was recorded as 203,302,031.

Remember, it was estimated that two and a half million people lived in the original thirteen colonies in 1776. We have to realize, of course, that the first official census was not until 1790, when more than five million people were recorded.

DANGER FROM ABOVE

Airplanes were a minor but increasingly important factor during the previous war, and the threat prompted changes to coastal defenses during the 1920s and 1930s. In fact, the Coast Artillery Corps was given the mission of designing and forming a doctrine for antiaircraft operations. Demonstrations in the 1920s by U.S. Army general Billy Mitchell showed the vulnerability of warships to air attack. He proved the beneficial use of aircraft for seacoast defenses against ships but also demonstrated the vulnerability of defenses against air power.

In the isolationist period of the United States, bombers were seen as more of a defense against naval attack than a strategic offensive weapon. However, planes like the Boeing B-17 Flying Fortress, which evolved as defensive weapons, turned out to have excellent offensive capacity as well.

But in those early days of the 1920s, Americans were tired of war. And those who lived in our area were tired of considering themselves to be in the enemy's bull's-eye. The Roaring Twenties were upon us; we were ready for a much-needed break and some fun in the sun.

16

THE TOURISTS

DON'T FORGET TO DANCE

People take pictures of the Summer, just in case someone thought they had missed it, and to prove that it really existed.

—*Ray Davies*

By the 1930s, America's population was 123 million people, and most people lived to be about sixty. You could buy a dozen eggs for forty-four cents, and milk was fourteen cents a quart. At the beginning of the 1930s, more than 15 million Americans—fully one quarter of all wage-earning workers—were unemployed. President Herbert Hoover did not do much to alleviate the crisis. Patience and self-reliance, he argued, were all Americans needed to get them through this "passing incident in our national lives."

Getting away from the heat and strife people suffered in the area was important, and entertainment—especially cheap entertainment—was sought after. These were the days when big bands and swing music were popular, like Duke Ellington, Benny Goodman and Glenn Miller.

Long before the New Jersey Turnpike or the Garden State Parkway were constructed to whisk tourists to Asbury Park for summer fun by the seashore, many seaside resorts in towns along the Atlantic Ocean and Raritan Bay were the primary destinations to be reached by train or by steamships.

The thirties were challenging, but people still found ways to have fun.

STATEN ISLAND

During the early twentieth century, the neighborhood of South Beach on Staten Island, New York, was full of summer bungalows and a beachfront lined with amusements, theaters, arcade games and rides. Families came from Manhattan, Sandy Hook and elsewhere to enjoy the festive resort community and the Franklin D. Roosevelt Boardwalk, known as the "Riviera of New York City."

Along with neighboring Midland Beach, South Beach was originally part of a small Dutch settlement in the mid-seventeenth century. Near the end of the nineteenth century, investors realized the potential of developing beachfront towns and so began building hotels, bathing pavilions, beer gardens, casinos, theaters and merry-go-rounds.

Before long, New Yorkers were going to this seaside retreat. Travel was easy, thanks to the Staten Island ferry from Manhattan and the various New Jersey ferries. South Beach was the terminus of a Staten Island railway line, which operated until 1953. Italian American immigrants made up a large part of South Beach's population at this time.

In 1906, the fifteen-acre Happyland Amusement Park was opened at the South Beach boardwalk. Since most Broadway theaters closed during the summer, Happyland filled the gap with stage productions and vaudeville shows, attracting more than thirty thousand visitors on the first day. Fire and animal shows were popular entertainment acts. Other amusements included the Canals of Venice, Japanese Tea Gardens, a skating rink and a shooting gallery.

The South Beach shore was very popular through the 1920s, but the Great Depression, along with fires and water pollution, eventually got the best of the community, and it became quite deserted. In 1935, the Works Progress Administration replaced the existing boardwalk with the Franklin Delano Roosevelt Boardwalk. The two-and-a-half-mile structure was built as part of a park that stretched from the Verrazano-Narrows Bridge to Miller Field.

Unfortunately, the time of Staten Island's South Beach has come and gone. The waterfront community south of the Verrazano-Narrows Bridge still has a classic old boardwalk, built in 1935. And there are still recreational facilities for baseball and hockey nearby, but priorities changed here. Similar to the eventual demise of Rockaway Beach, most of the amusements were gone by the 1970s. Several sections of neighborhoods along the shore were severely damaged in 2012 by Hurricane Sandy.

It's very doubtful this area will ever return to its glory days of the early twentieth century when Happyland Amusement Park brought a bit of Coney Island magic to the southern shore of Staten Island. Farther inland, real estate developers changed the landscape with planned communities that eventually appealed to New Yorkers of Italian, Irish and Hispanic descent.

KEANSBURG BOARDWALK

Meanwhile, across Raritan Bay in New Jersey, several waterfront resorts and adult playgrounds were being visited by people looking for a good time. Every town along the shores of New Jersey on Raritan Bayshore had its own carousel. And some towns had full-blown resorts.

There were several farsighted entrepreneurs in the day who saw the beaches of New Jersey as great places to lure tourists with recreational opportunities and then ultimately with land and houses they could purchase. One of these visionaries founded the Keansburg ferry service company in 1910 to lure New Yorkers who were interested in buying homes or vacationing in Keansburg. Eventually, the Keansburg Steamboat Company owned steamships to carry tourists to Keansburg. The company's pride and joy was the 231-foot-long *City Of Keansburg*.

From our boat in Raritan Bay, we can see a shipload of excited passengers, and we can hear music playing. It's because the steamship is preparing to dock at Keansburg, and a band is playing on board so people can dance and be entertained on their journey across Raritan Bay to have fun in the sun.

And after the passengers disembark onto a long pier extending into the bay, we can either walk down the pier where lots of people are fishing, or we can ride the length of the pier on a miniature train.

There were rides and amusements galore at this resort. And folks could stay in lots of different hotels or bungalows or even tents in campgrounds. Besides the rides, restaurants and a long boardwalk along the water's edge, there was the famous Crystal Pool with a kiddie pool and a waterfall.

Many people came to enjoy the beaches with their families. And in the good old summertime, there was nothing better on a hot day than to slip into Raritan Bay for a good soaking. And there were always plenty of lifeguards just in case.

If you didn't have a camera, there were always postcards to purchase. There was nothing like a day in Keansburg at the beach to help you forget your troubles in a period filled with difficulties.

Since 1917, Keansburg has had a colorful history and attracted visitors from Northern New Jersey and New York due to its convenient location. Starting as a fishing village and then later becoming a full-blown resort area for North Jersey and New York City visitors, Keansburg was in a strategic location as the closest shore destination stop along the Jersey Shore for folks traveling from the North.

Slowly, over time, Keansburg had fewer tourists coming, and the hotels began vanishing. Today, Keansburg is a ghost of what it once was. By the 1960s, Keansburg had transformed from a summer resort into a year-round town, with residential neighborhoods, schools and stores. The last steamship carried passengers to Keansburg in 1968—the flood of tourists had become a trickle.

Even so, the amusement park (referred to as the "boardwalk" by the locals) was a major attraction through the 1980s and today is trying to reclaim that identity. The park was renovated in 1995, and a water park was added to help bring the park back to its former glory. Today the Keansburg Amusement Park is once again a significant attraction, drawing in thousands of visitors from April to October.

HIGHLAND BEACH

Meanwhile, a slightly older resort took root near the entrance to Sandy Hook when the Reckless family purchased property in 1881. It was prime real estate stretching some fifty yards from the beach of the Atlantic Ocean to the shores on the Shrewsbury River.

By 1889, several seaside cottages had been built and sold on the northern side of Sandy Hook next to the Shrewsbury River. Cabanas had already been constructed as part of a private beach club. Many recreational activities, such as the Highland Beach Gravity Railroad (an early roller coaster), were also built.

Beachgoers came by steamships and by trains from everywhere. Highland Beach, located directly across from Highlands, New Jersey, had become a major resort comprising many different attractions and buildings in the Victorian style of architecture. There were the Bamboo Gardens,

Highland Beach in its heyday.

the Basket Pavilion dance hall, a Merry-Go-Round, bars and storefronts selling gifts and sundries.

Eventually, the Reckless family sold the property and Highland Beach to William Sandlass. He constructed the Bamboo Gardens, an outdoor theater called an Airdrome that was popular around World War I and the Bamboo Bar, where my parents went frequently.

Also on the property were private cottages and lots Sandlass leased to families who built cottages that they used each summer. Cabanas were constructed on the riverside of the peninsula. The Sandlass family lived in a house right in the middle of the roadway leading to Fort Hancock. It remained in this location until a hurricane damaged it in 1938. The Sandlass family then moved the house to a safer location closer to the Shrewsbury River.

Storms were always dangerous in the area and could cause considerable damage. For example, a storm in 1896 created a six-foot-deep inlet from the Atlantic Ocean to the Shrewsbury River. Water from the ocean rushed through the newly created channel with tremendous force, but when the wind shifted, the inlet began filling with sand. As a result, the north end of a row of bathhouses at Highland Beach was carried away. Even the large rocks that had been piled on the ocean side of the area to provide some protection were tossed about by the waves.

Highland Beach, which comprised the resort area, was later referred to as Sandlass Beach. It was patronized during the summer by residents of both

New Jersey and New York. However, by the 1930s, the nation's economy after the stock market crash of 1929 and the increasing threat of a future war abroad had forced many resorts to shift their focus.

Residents of Northern New Jersey and New York would usually take boats or the train to reach Highland Beach, but once train service was discontinued in the late 1940s and the automobile became the preferred method of travel with the opening of the New Jersey Turnpike and Garden State Parkway in the 1950s, public attention was drawn away from Highlands Beach as people began going to resorts farther south.

The Sandlass family was forced to change the focus of the resort by transforming it into the Sandlass Beach Club. It was an effort to refocus and attract families living in the northern Monmouth County area, instead of appealing only to tourists coming for just one day and then leaving.

The idea for highlighting the club worked for a while, and cabanas for patrons continued to be available. Eventually, the Victorian-style buildings were either torn down or converted to smaller, more useful buildings. All of the private cottages remained on the northern edge of the Sandlass property.

By 1974, the U.S. Army had decommissioned and closed Fort Hancock. It then gave the land to the Department of the Interior as part of Gateway National Recreation Area. A new highway ramp was built off the bridge, which went from Highlands to Sandy Hook and Sea Bright.

Today, as tourists and beachgoers cross the bridge to enjoy the beaches, they may see the dilapidated home where the Sandlass family once lived. Efforts are underway to restore the house as a museum to share the relics and history of the grand resorts that once existed.

THE BENNYS ARE COMING, THE BENNYS ARE COMING

Space tourism is a logical outgrowth of the adventure tourist market.
—*astronaut Buzz Aldrin*

If you live in the area of New Jersey, then you know the definition of *Benny*. It's a somewhat pejorative name for a tourist. So how did the term originate? One prevailing theory says it originated from an acronym that was stamped on train tickets held by tourists headed for the beach. In other words, BENNY represents the towns where they boarded the train to reach the shore, such as Bayonne, Elizabeth, Newark and New York (BENNY).

A less popular theory says the term may have originated from the early twentieth-century practice of wealthy New Yorkers taking trips to the Jersey Shore as treatment for maladies such as anemia, hemophilia and hysteria. These therapeutic trips were called beneficials. Often, visitors would claim to be at the Jersey Shore on a beneficial, hence the derivative Benny.

Another theory is that the word was used to identify New Yorkers who came down to the shore and flashed wads of $100 bills with a picture of Ben "Benny" Franklin on the front of them.

Regardless of the origin, the Bennys come every summer to this area, which results in a lot more traffic on the highways and local roads. On the plus side, however, they do spend money.

QUEEN OF THE WAVES

I am not a person who reaches for the moon as long as I have the stars.
—Gertrude Ederle

Gertrude Caroline Ederle trained in the Shrewsbury River, Sandy Hook Bay, Raritan Bay and even New York Harbor in preparation for her goal to be the first woman to swim across the English Channel, which she achieved in 1926 at the age of twenty-one.

While she was born in New York City, her father taught her to swim in Highlands, New Jersey, where her family owned a summer cottage.

Before her world-renowned accomplishment, she won many national and world swimming championships, including a gold medal at the 1924 Summer Olympics in Paris. The following year, she began to prepare for her biggest challenge—crossing the English Channel. As soon as she returned home from Paris, she swam the twenty-two miles from Battery Park in New York City to Sandy Hook. It took her seven hours and eleven minutes, which beat all records of the day. She would frequently train in the Shrewsbury River by swimming against the current, which was one of the fastest currents in the area.

Ederle had tried to cross the English Channel once before, but she had failed in the attempt. For her second attempt at crossing the Channel, Ederle had an entourage aboard a tugboat: her father and her sister Meg,

Gertrude Ederle.

as well as a writer for the *New York Daily News*, the paper that sponsored Ederle's swim.

During her twelfth hour at sea, her trainer had become so concerned by unfavorable winds that he called "Gertie, you must come out!" Ederle lifted her head from the choppy waters and replied, "What for?"

Only five men had been able to swim the English Channel before Ederle. The best time had been sixteen hours and thirty-three minutes. Ederle completed her swim in fourteen hours and thirty-four minutes.

When Ederle returned home, she was greeted with a ticker-tape parade in Manhattan, with more than two million people lining the streets to cheer her. In Highlands, the town where she trained, she was honored later in life with the establishment of the Gertrude Ederle Park, which overlooks the Shrewsbury River, where she swam against the current. At the Twin Lights of Navesink, also in Highlands, the Historical Society of Highlands has an exhibit on her accomplishments.

Today, an annual swim is held from New York City's Battery Park to Sandy Hook in honor of the Queen of the Waves.

17

THE BUILDERS

I don't ever think about the roads I didn't take
because I spend too much time thinking what's ahead. I don't go backwards.
—*Kelli O'Hara*

LENAPE FOOTPATHS

Okay, let's give credit where credit is due for the road system in New York and New Jersey: The Lenape Indians. Yup, they established some terrific footpaths throughout our area, which of course, we eventually had to pave over and then lose all memory of their contributions to our road system. The British have to share the blame with us because they created several roads in and between the colonies. Or, more precisely, they built the Kings Highway. Neither the Lenape Indians nor the Brits were going sixty-plus miles per hour down their respective routes, so we had to pave over everything. Ah, progress.

COLONIAL TRAVEL GUIDE

Most of the colonial folks traveled from place to place by walking where they wanted to go, and sometimes they used the footpaths left by the Lenape Indians. If they had to travel a long distance, it was usually only to get supplies or to visit people because it got lonely in the colonial hinterlands. The poor rarely went anywhere.

Another way to travel was by horse if you owned one. In fact, one of the first things a colonist would buy is a horse for travel, pleasure or to help with work on a farm, although mules were more adept at helping to plow fields and haul stuff in wagons.

Some people could also get themselves a vehicle with wheels. For example, farmers used wagons for work on the farm and to deliver their goods to merchants in town for sale or trade. Or some folks had a carriage a horse might pull for a nice ride into the next village.

If you had to cross a river or bay, a boat was utilized, and it was either a boat with oars to row or sails to catch the wind. Of course, the Lenape Indians used their dugout canoes to travel by water.

THE KING'S HIGHWAY

Before the Dutch arrived, many Lenape trails ran the entire length of the island (New York City), such as parts of today's Broadway. When the Dutch finally arrived, they had decided that this particular trail would be Heere Wegh, which is Dutch for "Broad Way." The first paved street in New York was Brouwer Street (Stone Street) in 1658.

Giving credit where credit is due, the British were terrific road builders, as exemplified with the Kings Highway.

For the most part, people think that King's Highway runs from Perth Amboy, New Jersey, to Salem, New Jersey. This is mostly true, with some distinctions. The road toward Amboy can be seen on a 1677 map of Burlington as "Old Indian Road." Generally, because the state was separated into East New Jersey and West New Jersey, Old Indian Road was an excellent road to take between both provinces.

Eventually, the two distinct provinces were surrendered to Queen Anne in 1703. That's when the so-called Jerseys became an official royal colony. So, most of the folks who took the road by horse or carriage in those days referred to it as Queen's Highway. Remember Ben Franklin's son, William? Well, he was escorted on this road by the militia.

The entire King's Highway, built from 1650 to 1735 by orders of Charles II of England, was 1,300 miles long and connected Charleston, South Carolina, to Boston, Massachusetts.

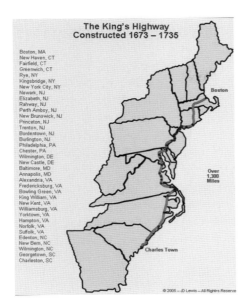

The King's Highway.

Today, the King's Highway Historic District in New Jersey covers the portions of U.S. Route 206 and New Jersey Route 27 that connect Lawrenceville with Kingston in Franklin Township and South Brunswick through to Princeton.

In New York, early records indicate Governor Peter Stuyvesant of the New Amsterdam colony first referred to it as "Highway" in a grant dating from 1654. Later, it became known as the Cross Road.

FERRY SERVICE

By 1642, the first regular ferry service in New York Harbor was running between the two villages of New Amsterdam (Manhattan) and Breuckelen (Brooklyn) with a combined population of less than one thousand.

If you lived in New Amsterdam and looked toward Breuckelen, you saw some structures by the shore next to where the Brooklyn Bridge was built much later. There also was a high bluff that came to be known as Brooklyn Heights, where some of the Dutch settlers lived. Incidentally, this site was also known as "Brookland Ferry" when General George Washington quickly left after the Battle of Long Island.

The ferryman would also take passengers across the harbor in exchange for wampum, which was crafted by the Lenape Indians as decorative necklaces composed of white and purple beads from the quahog (hard-shelled clam). Wampum became the most popular form of currency, used in both the Dutch settlements and with the Lenape themselves.

By 1654, there were numerous ferry services, so the city officials issued licenses to ferry operators. By 1709, Christopher Billop had begun his own ferry service, which crossed the Arthur Kill from Tottenville on Staten Island to Perth Amboy, New Jersey. If you remember, Billop owned the Conference House, where some well-known Patriots met with the British to try and prevent the Revolutionary War.

When the Dutch named the island Nieuw Amsterdam (New Amsterdam), they fully utilized the waterways that surrounded them. For example, one of the earliest canals built was one following the route of today's Broad Street. They also built a pier into the East River from Moore Street. In 1661, they founded the Communipaw ferry, which crossed the Hudson River to Jersey City.

The Fulton Ferry became the first steamship ferry to cross the East River and connect Manhattan with Brooklyn. The Fulton Ferry Company was established by Robert Fulton in 1814. Ferry trips now took about twelve minutes, and there was much less chance for the ferry to succumb to currents or wind.

While ferries were the solution for people who had to cross one of our many waterways in the early days, they could not take you outside of Raritan Bay and into the Atlantic Ocean. If you were going farther, like to one of the towns along the coastline or across the ocean, a ship would be the answer. However, during the early seventeenth century, a voyage across the ocean was still dangerous and took six to eight weeks depending on the weather. In fact, traveling by ship was fraught with other dangers, such as sickness, disease, being shipwrecked and raids by pirates. Sounds like a fun-filled voyage.

GET ME TO THE BEACH

As those newfangled automobiles began selling like hotcakes, folks from New York City and other parts of New Jersey wanted to drive to the beaches of New York and New Jersey. To accommodate their desire, New Jersey began building a bridge in 1910 over the mouth of the Raritan River. Within years of its completion, however, it was deemed inadequate to handle not only increasing traffic but also the weight of larger trucks. By 1916, the Victory Bridge had been erected to meet growing demand. Unfortunately, the new cars were being brought to the beaches of New Jersey in droves. Also, more and more boaters were traveling up and down the Raritan River, so the traffic had to stop while the bridge was raised so boats could pass through. It was evident to everyone that instead of replacing the existing bridge, a new fixed bridge would be added; it had to be high enough to allow any boat to travel under it without impeding traffic flow.

The work on the new bridge began in 1935 as traffic on Route 35 and Route 4 was rerouted into a new traffic circle in South Amboy. Three workers were killed when they fell from the bridge during construction. Five years later, the bridge was opened to traffic. The Thomas A. Edison Bridge, became known locally as the Route 35 Extension from the Woodbridge Cloverleaf to Keyport. Most people, however, referred to it as the Perth Amboy Bypass.

Construction of the Garden State Parkway began in 1946, and by 1950, only 10 miles of the parkway's 165-mile route had opened. At this slow rate, some government officials were concerned it might take another forty years before completion. Therefore, funding was speeded up, and before long, the Garden State Parkway was completed by 1953 with two hundred entrance and exit ramps.

In 1952, the New Jersey Highway Authority mandated that the Garden State Parkway be constructed quickly to relieve the traffic congestion in New Jersey. The project was to include a bridge for the Garden State Parkway to continue over the Raritan River at Perth Amboy. It would be named the Alfred E. Driscoll Bridge in honor of a former governor of New Jersey. The Driscoll Bridge was to be the largest of the almost three hundred bridges in the Garden State Parkway system. It was designed as a nearly identical twin of the Edison Bridge because of the boating clearance requirements.

While the New Jersey Turnpike was designed to move traffic through the state, the Garden State Parkway was built to efficiently move local traffic from one place to another. For example, the turnpike was built with very few exits and sent mostly interstate traffic from one end of the state to the other. The Garden State Parkway was designed with lots of local exits.

New Jersey officials assembled a team of leading engineers and consultants to examine state-of-the-art highway designs, bridge planning and new technology. For example, the Garden State Parkway was built to anticipate future traffic conditions. They anticipated higher speeds eventually, so they included banked curves to handle the increased speeds more safely. They also constructed wider medians and shoulders to build additional lanes if

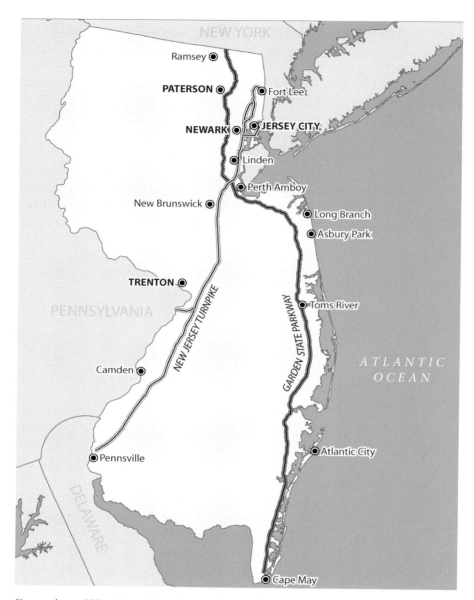

Comparison of New Jersey Turnpike and Garden State Parkway.

future traffic warranted. Additional concrete was poured into the bridge foundations so they could be widened more efficiently at a future date. All of these future-oriented features saved millions of dollars in taxes.

The Garden State Parkway was mostly opened by 1954. Two years later, the Garden State Parkway was fully completed with the opening of the Great Egg Harbor Bridge.

By 1957, a nine-mile extension connected the Garden Staten Parkway to the New York State Thruway. Eventually, in 1964, the Verrazano-Narrows Bridge was completed with a span of more than four thousand feet—the longest suspended span in the world at the time. In 2003, *Queen Mary 2*, once the world's largest passenger ships, passed under the bridge during high tide with thirteen feet between it and the bridge. It was a close call, for sure.

BRICK BY BRICK

All in all, you're just another brick in the wall.

—*Roger Waters*

By the middle of the nineteenth century, we were building bridges, tunnels and roads like crazy. We were also constructing buildings for lots of businesses. And the building block of the day was the good old-fashioned brick. Luckily, massive clay deposits in and around Raritan Bay provided the essential ingredients for this vital building block. The mud and clay drew thousands of immigrant workers into the brickmaking industry, and up went buildings all around us.

Meanwhile, the Sayre & Fisher Brick Company, founded in Wood's Landing (Sayreville), New Jersey, in 1850, steadily grew into the largest brick manufacturer in the world. It was ideally located next to the Raritan River, where barges could carry the bricks into Raritan Bay and then wherever else they were needed.

A man-made one-mile-long Washington Canal was dug and completed in 1831 to shorten the time it took to carry clay, sand and bricks from the villages of Old Bridge and Washington (present-day Borough of South River) to the Sayre & Fisher Brick Company on the Raritan River.

The founders of the company, James Sayre of Newark and Peter Fisher of New York City, were competing against a large number of companies making bricks in the area. By 1878, however, Sayre & Fisher was producing

SAYRE & FISHER'S NEW PLANT

Sayreville Brick Factory.

178 million bricks every year, and they were used to build many of the houses in central New Jersey. In fact, Sayre & Fisher bricks built the pedestal on which the Statue of Liberty stands. The plant closed in 1960, but by then, it had produced an estimated 6 billion bricks. One of the smokestacks can still be seen on Main Street in Sayreville.

Today, Sayreville's clay deposits remain one of the world's largest sources of museum-quality fossils found in amber (prehistoric tree resin), which captured many species of various insects and plants living almost 100 million years ago.

Brickmaking flourished, but industries of nearly every kind utilized the Raritan River because of its easy access to an abundant water supply and the convenience of a variety of transportation to some of the largest markets in the country.

Sayreville was not the only location where brick factories were successful. There were, in fact, many factories in the area during the heyday of using bricks for building.

Another successful company was National Fireproofing Company, which existed until the 1930s. This company mined clay mud rich in alumina and silica, which helped create heat-resistant bricks used for insulation, ceramics and ovens.

One of the company's clay mines was located in Union Beach, New Jersey, next to Raritan Bay. You can actually see the mine today, but it's completely filled with water. Why? It's a funny story, actually.

Back in the 1930s, they were actively removing clay from the mine using draglines, bulldozers and dump trucks. One of the devices used to remove the clay accidentally uncovered an underground spring, which started flooding the bottom of the open mine. The miners tried to pump out the water, but it was coming in faster than their pumps could remove it.

Dragline in Natco Clay pit before filling up with water.

Natco Lake in Union Beach, New Jersey.

Meanwhile, they frantically tried to move equipment out of the mine and to safety before it all flooded.

Eventually, one member of the crew came up with the idea of draining the water by digging a ditch to nearby Thorne's Creek, which happened to flow into Raritan Bay. Unfortunately, these folks didn't really understand how the tides of Raritan Bay and Thorne's Creek would affect their efforts to drain the mine. The water started to flow into the creek initially, but the tidal creek crested later in the day and filled the pit with seawater from the brackish creek.

They were doomed. One dragline could not be recovered during the flooding. You can actually still see it sometimes at low tide. The company considered how much it would cost to permanently drain the mine against the declining value of clay and the life cycle of the mine. They eventually abandoned the site and sold the property surrounding it.

Today, the flooded mine is called Natco Lake. State Route 36, which is the main road bringing tourists to Sandy Hook, crosses the center of the lake. There are several trails throughout the area comprising Natco Lake and portions of Thorne's Creek.

18

THE DRINKERS

WATER ON THE ROCKS

Prohibition is better than no liquor at all.

—*Will Rogers*

Reverend Samuel Lockwood of Keyport, New Jersey, warned that alcohol would rob people of their brains. He explained in 1854: "Quick as fire it causes the crimson current to rush through every vein—like electricity it flies through every silver nerve—suffusing the brain, magnetizing the mind, and blurring the vision, becrimsoning the cheek, making garrulous the tongue, fretting the passions, and setting in a flame the lust." Yikes! I'm definitely on the wagon.

Fifteen years later, in 1869, the National Prohibition Party was formed. It would coordinate campaigns that eventually led to a constitutional ban on the production, importation, transportation and sale of alcoholic beverages from 1920 to 1933. How delightful!

The decision to outlaw the production, transportation and distribution of alcohol did not catch on immediately. A lot of cities and states were slow in reacting to the enforcement of the law.

The so-called Liquor Center of America was New York City. And while the entire area surrounding Raritan Bay was profoundly affected, the immigrant population in New York City was unhappy about not drinking.

Along with continual raids by the police and the Mafia smuggling liquor, Manhattan became a crazy town. What else is new?!

New York City never really accepted Prohibition as a law. Oh, laws were passed, and the police were trained to enforce them, but the City of Immigrants never budged from its right to drink alcohol.

What people started to realize was writing a law and then enforcing it were two different things. So, the government created the Bureau of Prohibition to fight the war on manufacturing alcohol and the consumption of it. It was moderately successful but stimulated more smuggling of liquor and speakeasies throughout the country where it could be consumed.

Unfortunately, the federal agents were not trained well enough to enforce the laws of Prohibition, nor were they adequately paid. As a result, many of the agents accepted bribes. Even the U.S. Coast Guard was "on the take," as they say. In fact, the bootleggers viewed bribery as a business expense.

By the end of the first year since the creation of the New York bureau, at least half of the two hundred new agents were fired. Even the state director resigned because he said it was a "hopeless and thankless" job.

Many historians believe Prohibition led to the Roaring Twenties, and that's when the Mafia raised its ugly head by creating Italian rum-shipping ports. Many Italian and Sicilian families saw an opportunity, so they started importing alcohol from other countries. It didn't take very long for the Mafia's business to grow, and soon the speakeasies could make some $5,000 every week. Good money in the 1920s.

Meanwhile, across Raritan Bay and along the Shrewsbury River and Sandy Hook Bay, the people who worked on the water during the day, such as fishermen and clammers, became the bootleggers, rumrunners and smugglers who retrieved liquor in cases on boats in the Atlantic Ocean and brought them back to grateful business owners in Highlands, New Jersey, and other towns. In many of these towns, rumrunning and bootlegging were a way of life.

Author Muriel J. Smith recounts one of the more famous stories of the era: a murder right in the center of one New Jersey town. According to Smith, a local newspaper reported that Frank LeConte of Newark was well known in the rumrunning business. It seems Frank argued with Robert Schneider, who was also successful in the same illegal activity. Robert accused Frank of disrupting the delivery of illicit alcohol and wanted to settle the score.

One night in Highlands, Robert spotted Frank and then pursued him as he left town and went to Atlantic Highlands. As Frank tried to escape, his vehicle was blocked by a train at the station. Robert and his men jumped out of their vehicle and put a bullet in Frank's stomach. When it was all over, Frank LeConte and at least six others were treated at the hospital in Long Branch, and a whole lot of them were charged with various crimes.

Unfortunately, two days after the attack, Frank LeConte died at the hospital. Because no witnesses were willing to describe what happened, everyone involved went back to their same old routine of doing what they did best—smuggling liquor.

In 1917, around the time we were fighting Germany during World War I, and three years before national Prohibition took effect, there was a bitter debate between two New Jersey communities that were joined at the hip: the Methodist religious campground of Ocean Grove and the neighboring resort city of Asbury Park.

A New Jersey law from 1896 stated that intoxicating liquor could not be sold within one mile of a religious camp, meaning that Asbury Park, which bordered Ocean Grove, was required by law to be dry.

The Anti-Saloon League, which fought for Prohibition, suspected that the law was being ignored in Asbury Park, and so it hired someone to investigate. The investigator reported there was prostitution, intoxication, voter fraud, gambling and corruption in Asbury Park—and all of this illegal activity was supported by the mayor, the chief of police and other leaders of Asbury Park. The Anti-Saloon League published a pamphlet that described the corruption, but before long, national Prohibition became the law of the land.

In 1920, the Volstead Act was passed to support the enforcement of the Eighteenth Amendment by prohibiting the manufacture, sale, or transportation of intoxicating liquors. However, the act did not expressly prohibit the consumption of liquor. Therefore, people were mostly encouraged and determined to obtain liquor, in spite of the law.

New Jersey, Connecticut and Rhode Island resisted Prohibition. In 1922, New Jersey became the last state to ratify it. In fact, New Jersey earned the nickname "Bootlegger's Paradise." The word *bootlegger* originated with rum smugglers who would hide a bottle of illegal liquor inside their large rain boots.

Many of the towns along Raritan Bay became ports where smugglers would bring the illicit alcohol to those willing to buy it. While rumrunning was common along New Jersey's coast during the 1920s, New York Bay became known as "rum row."

The Jersey skiff, designed and built in Highlands at King Boat Works, became the boat of choice among smugglers. It had the speed and strength required to outrun the Coast Guard gunboats. The smugglers would depart during the night to meet ships located a few miles from the coastline with a fresh cargo of rum from the Caribbean or whiskey from Canada.

After the smugglers picked up their valuable cargo, they would race back to the buyers who were waiting in secret tunnels and rooms in towns along Raritan Bay. In those days, a case of whiskey from Canada might cost about $7, but they could sell it for $500 in the public market.

Homes and restaurants along Raritan Bay stored their illegal liquor in burlap bags in secret rooms or under floorboards. Some people and businesses even had their own stills to make liquor.

Captain William "Bill" McCoy was a pioneer rumrunner. He had a reputation as an honest dealer, and his fleet of ships was known all along the Atlantic coast of America as well as Canada. Many smugglers would cut their illegal liquor with water to increase their profits, but Bill McCoy was renowned for not diluting. As a result of his reputation, he became known as the "Real McCoy," even though the phrase did not originate with him. Unfortunately, the Coast Guard captured his ship in 1924. He went on trial in Newark, New Jersey, and served a nine-month sentence in the Essex County jail.

A lot of folks who were against Prohibition argued that too many people were being killed by overeager police officers and others who tried to bring smugglers to justice. For example, twenty-four-year-old Gerard "Gerry" Kadenbach was one of those victims; he was alone in his boat and killed by an unidentified crew member of the Coast Guard.

There was no liquor found on Kadenbach's high-speed boat, nor did anyone witness him dumping booze into the water. Unfortunately, if you had a speedy boat, you might be suspected as a rumrunner. Kadenbach's family had owned a hardware store in Highlands, and Gerry worked there. He was a volunteer fireman.

In 1925, Keyport, New Jersey, was another town active in smuggling liquor, as well. George Pease was a butcher who owned a seventeen-room house in Keyport. The police chief of Keyport confronted Pease at home in 1925.

Historian Jack Jeandron said that Pease "pulled out two or three $500 bills from his pocket and offered to wager it against $2 that he had no liquor in the house." There was none.

Before long, however, the police chief saw Pease moving some seventy-five cases of liquor from a room to his back porch. He assigned one of his officers to watch from a neighbor's house. By the time the police chief came back, most of the liquor had disappeared. Nobody was ever charged with breaking any law.

Those were just examples of how difficult Prohibition was for ordinary people and for the folks who tried to enforce it. As a result, Prohibition was falling apart. The nation was falling into an economic depression, and serious crime was increasing everywhere. The only people who seemed to be making money in those days were people in the illegal liquor production, sale and consumption business.

Mafioso Lucky Luciano, who was the Mafia boss in our area, made more money from illegal liquor than almost any other business.

It was becoming evident to lawmakers that illegal activity in the liquor business was profitable. More importantly, they started realizing no taxes were being paid. Before Prohibition, almost 15 percent of government income was derived from the sale of alcohol. These things always come down to money. It was either spend more money to enforce Prohibition or kill the law and then reinstate the federal tax on alcohol. Why didn't I think of that?

So, in 1933, Congress came up with the Twenty-First Amendment, which repealed the Eighteenth Amendment. Done. Prohibition was over. Let's crack open that bottle of Champagne in the cooler in my boat. Yes, we're still in the boat.

19

THE FLYERS

FLYING BOATS

Being able to land in the water gives me lots of liquid runways along the shores.
—Jimmy Buffet

The Aeromarine Plane and Motor Company was an early American aircraft manufacturer in Keyport, New Jersey, that operated from 1914 to 1930. Aeromarine mostly built military seaplanes and flying boats. The company broke new ground in aviation by offering some of the first regularly scheduled flights. In 1928, the firm renamed itself Aeromarine-Klemm Corporation; it remained in business until the Great Depression forced its closure in 1930.

LOOK, IT'S A BIRD. IT'S A PLANE. IT'S THE *HINDENBURG*!

It's smoke, and it's flames now…and the frame is crashing to the ground, not quite to the mooring-mast. Oh, the humanity and all the passengers screaming.
—Herbert Morrison, broadcaster

In May 1937, a group of boys were swimming on the banks of the Shrewsbury River in Highlands, New Jersey. When they looked up, they saw

One of many seaplanes built by Aeromarine.

Hindenburg over New York City.

the *Hindenburg*, which was heading toward the Lakehurst Naval Air Station. One of the boys later became my father, and he said it was flying so low to the river he could see a woman staring at him from one of the windows. She waved at him, and he waved back. Little did he know what was in store for the woman, along with the other thirty-five passengers and sixty-one crew members at the end of their fateful journey.

Unfortunately, on the day of the tragedy, there was a report of afternoon thunderstorms when and where the airship was supposed to dock. The captain decided to delay the docking until the weather cleared, so he charted his course over New York City, which was sensational for the people on the ground. Then he passed over Raritan Bay and headed toward the mouth of the Shrewsbury River, where those young boys would spot it passing by. Finally, when the weather cleared, the captain headed to the docking station and, by early evening, slowly made the final descent. As they descended and the mooring lines were tossed down to the ground crew, a few witnesses saw part of the fabric exterior flutter as if gas were leaking. Suddenly, the *Hindenburg* caught fire and quickly became engulfed in flames. Many passengers and crew survived, but thirty-six people were killed.

Fire departments from the local area and beyond were called to extinguish the fire, but it was far too late. Even firefighters from towns along Raritan Bay rushed to the scene to offer help. Today, a girder-like piece of the *Hindenburg*—along with pictures and newspapers—may be seen at the Fire Museum on Broad Street in Keyport, New Jersey.

20

THE FIGHTERS

THE BIG ONE

We shall fight on the beaches, we shall fight on the landing grounds, we shall fight in the fields and in the streets, we shall fight in the hills; we shall never surrender.

—*Winston Churchill*

Just before the start of World War II in 1939, the Army Signal Corps arrived at the Twin Lights lighthouse to conduct some tests of long-range radar. Equipment developed at Fort Monmouth in New Jersey was set up near the north tower. The top-secret tests were conducted, and then the equipment was quietly removed. However, a local newspaper got wind of the test, and the next day a headline declared that a so-called Mystery Ray had been tested.

Radar would be critical, especially after Germany invaded Poland on September 1, 1939, to start a war that would eventually be described as the "Big One."

As for the United States, we looked on in horror for the second time in a generation as the Germans reignited their lust for conquest. In September 1940, Fort Hancock on Sandy Hook shook off the peace and quiet of the Depression and roared back to life as America activated nearly thirty National Guard coast artillery regiments and infantry divisions and then enacted America's first peacetime draft. A massive building program sprang up to house the newly arrived soldiers, who quickly went to work on the fort's guns, many of which hadn't been fired in years.

Fort Hancock also served as a mobilization center with a tent city and lots of temporary buildings for new recruits who would train before going overseas to fight in World War II. Eventually, when my dad turned eighteen, he would be one of the new recruits.

During the war, Germany would invade ten more countries. Adolf Hitler was even considering an attack against the United States. His plan would have utilized long-range Messerschmitt bombers, which in theory could fly from the Azores (an autonomous region of Portugal) to America. Ironically, Hitler named his planes *America Bombers*. His plan required him to capture the Azores, which he never did, and he built only one so-called America Bomber.

After Pearl Harbor was attacked on December 7, 1941, the United States declared war against Japan. Germany and Italy declared war on us, and we responded in kind. Now the world really was at war barely twenty years after the previous one had ended. The so-called War in the Pacific was of less concern to people living in our area, however. It wasn't for lack of care or patriotism. We were just far more concerned with a genuine threat at our front door. We were afraid of the German navy coming across the Atlantic Ocean to attack us. Once again, German submarines arrived on our doorstep and the Jersey Shore.

Admiral Karl Dönitz was the commander of Germany's U-boat fleet. "Operation Drumbeat," the U-boat offensive against U.S. merchant shipping, began in January 1942 within a month of the Japanese attack on the American Pacific Fleet at Pearl Harbor, Hawaii. Dönitz's U-boats operated up and down the Eastern Seaboard, from Maine to Florida and into the Gulf of Mexico. Germany also believed one of its U-boats could "steam directly into the throat of New York Harbor, on the surface, at night, without being challenged." Sure, right.

Some of Germany's military leaders believed America's submarine nets and batteries of guns were ineffective. Dönitz wasn't even confident our defensives were real. In 1941, however, he was somewhat correct in his assumption. Unfortunately, even though our testing of radar proved it would work, we weren't yet fully up to speed with our radar capabilities. Even the technology we required to detect U-boats underwater wouldn't be available until 1942. Furthermore, radar of the day had a limited range.

U-boat Alley, as it was called, was generally located off our coastlines of New York and New Jersey. The first freighter to be sunk was the SS *Cyclops* near Nova Scotia. Next, another attack took place a little closer to home, near New York. The U-boat torpedoed the SS *Norness*, which was sixty miles from Montauk Point, Long Island. Both ships met their fate at the hands of *U-123* under the command of Korvettenkapitän Reinhard Hardegen.

The evening after sinking the *Norness*, *U-123* started cruising along the south shore of Long Island toward New York City. Because the U-boat's crew didn't have accurate navigational charts of the area, they almost crash-landed on Rockaway shore. From reports retrieved later, the U-boat may have also come close to beaches on the shores of Fort Tilden or Jacob Riis Beach. By about 10:00 p.m., the German captain was looking at the lighted buildings of New York City through his periscope. Later, he also saw the parachute jump and Wonder Wheel of Coney Island. Unfortunately, the lookouts at Fort Tilden were in the one-hundred-foot-tall fire-control towers but couldn't see a thing.

The U-boat finally steered away from New York City and came across a target. It was a British tanker. They were about sixty miles east of Ambrose light and certainly within sight of the folks who lived on the south shore of Long Island. The U-boat fired and sank the ship, then turned south toward the Delaware Bay along the New Jersey shore.

Freighters were always targets of German U-boats in 1942. *National Archives.*

There were just a few German U-boats responsible for the sinking of some 397 ships in the first six months of 1942. There were 171 ships sunk off the Atlantic coast from Maine to Florida, 62 sunk in the Gulf of Mexico, and 141 in the Caribbean. A total of 2,403 persons were killed and 1,178 were wounded.

Explosions could be heard and burning wrecks could be seen from the shorelines of New Jersey and Long Island at night. Dead bodies, debris and oil washed ashore on many East Coast beaches. Those living in the coastal zones had a front-row seat to the grim realities of war.

Despite all of this, blackouts were not implemented quickly enough while the U-boats silently cruised along the coast of our country. U-boats could see cargo ships moving along the coast at night, even though they usually cruised with their lights off. Nevertheless, lights on our shores were still lit, and they could see the outline of ships against the coastal lights.

Eventually, orders were given to towns along the shore to turn down the lights at night. Even with lights dimmed or turned off completely, you could still see the glow of New York City from twenty-five miles away.

We started getting more serious about the dangers closer to home. That's why a campaign started with slogans like: "Loose Lips Sink Ships." The purpose, of course, was to prevent German spies from hearing public conversations and passing it on to Germany and to the U-boats. While helping to stem the flow of information, the campaign did little to prevent U-boats from attacking ships out on the high seas. They would simply wait offshore, intercept ship radio transmissions to locate potential targets and then torpedo any large ship that they could see through their periscopes. By the middle of 1942, the U.S. Navy started using many new techniques and technologies to prevent submarines from attacking ships.

German U-boats were also used to deliver secret agents to our beaches. In fact, you may have heard about the four saboteurs who snuck into our country via U-boat. They simply strolled into Amagansett, Long Island, on June 13, 1942. Three days later, four more landed in Ponte Vedra, Florida, on June 16, 1942.

They were armed with explosives and planned to blow up factories, bridges, tunnels, power plants and other public works. One member of the group eventually turned himself in to the FBI and confessed everything. All eight of the saboteurs were eventually arrested and tried, with six of them executed in Washington, D.C., less than two months after stepping off the U-boat. Director of the FBI J. Edgar Hoover said of the incident: "The recent landing of saboteurs from Nazi submarines sounded a new alert for all Americans. They were apprehended before they could carry out their plans of destruction."

According to a book by Samuel Eliot Morison, *The Battle of the Atlantic*, one particular German submarine, *U-608*, was able to place ten submerged mines in New York Harbor on November 10, 1942. A minesweeping boat discovered one of the first mines, and subsequently, New York Harbor was closed for forty-eight hours. Actually, it was the only time during the entire war when the harbor was ever closed.

We were behind schedule in getting our nation's defenses ready for a war we tried to avoid, and we were quite unprepared for the German invasion of U-boats. Now we were furiously developing better coastal defenses, especially after U-boats were successfully attacking ships in our shallow coastal waters.

By 1943, a Harbor Entrance Control Post was built on top of Battery Potter at Fort Hancock. Three stories in height, it was the tallest and largest structure at Fort Hancock and had been converted to a sizeable fire-control platform to aim the guns.

The underground bunkers of the antiquated Sandy Hook Mortar Battery on Sandy Hook were converted into the Harbor Defense Command Post. The two-gun batteries that launched America's modern era of defense, each forty-five years old, were still hard at work protecting New York Harbor. In fact, all of the forts surrounding New York City were working hard to install the minefield, underwater detection systems and antiaircraft guns and constructing new gun batteries.

Protection against air attack was quick to evolve, however. Existing gun batteries were camouflaged, but if detected, they remained vulnerable to air attack. The first batteries of heavy guns constructed after World War I were mostly open to reveal the guns inside. Every gun battery was camouflaged with netting and vegetation to avoid detection from the sea and the air. Several batteries were modernized under thick concrete casemates and covered with vegetation to make them virtually invisible from above and well protected against bombing. Antiaircraft batteries sprang up everywhere, from the shores of Fort Hancock to the rooftops of New York City skyscrapers.

Guns were also mounted on mobile railroad cars so they could be moved from one location to another by utilizing all of the public railroad tracks throughout the country. Sea mines, searchlights, radar and antiaircraft guns supplemented our coastal defenses as the war progressed.

Private and commercial boaters were sent this message: "A mined area covering the approaches to New York Harbor has been established. Incoming

Some guns were mounted on a train so they could be moved easily.

Laying mines in New York Harbor.

vessels will secure directions for safe navigation from patrol vessels stationed off Ambrose Channel Entrance."

Just like we did during the First World War, we installed a submarine net across the Narrows. Also, a couple of marine barges were stationed at the nets and were moved by tugboats when necessary to allow ships to enter. Each barge had a power generator for electricity. One of the barges had hydrophones, which could detect approaching U-boats. The barges were also equipped with one .50-caliber and two .30-caliber machine guns. The other barge was armed with Thompson machine guns.

Meanwhile, the coast artillery units of the army spent a lot of energy developing weapons to prevent surface ships from attacking, but no ships ever came to attack our shores. By now, Germany knew all too well that our defenses would be effective against them.

While New York Harbor continued to be an idealized target for Germany, many U-boats had become reluctant to navigate through the strong tides and prevalent shoals of the bays, harbor or rivers of our area. Advanced technology allowed the United States and its allies to hunt down and sink U-boats—often with the loss of their entire crews.

Fort Hancock's population peaked during World War II at more than seven thousand soldiers.

WAY OUT THERE

Every ship needs a port because unlike ships waves never get tired.
—Mehmet Murat ildan

Naval Weapons Station Earle is a U.S. Navy base in Monmouth County. It includes an almost-three-mile pier into Sandy Hook Bay, where ammunition can be loaded and unloaded from warships at a safe distance from densely populated areas.

The station is divided into two sections: 1) Mainside, located in parts of Colts Neck Township, Howell Township, Wall Township and Tinton Falls; and 2) Waterfront Area, which includes the pier complex in Sandy Hook Bay located in the Leonardo section of Middletown Township. The two areas are connected by fifteen-mile Normandy Road and a private rail line.

Naval Weapons Station Earle Pier Complex in Raritan Bay (Digital Collections/PTC).

Naval operations related to World War II demanded an ammunition depot near the greater New York metropolitan area but away from areas with large populations. When an ammunition ship caught fire while moored in Bayonne, New Jersey, plans were accelerated to locate a site for a pier that could load ammunition without worrying too much about damaging property or injuring civilians. They chose Sandy Hook Bay, which would be safe and sheltered. Ships could accept ammunition by rail lines, which extended to the end of the pier. As a result, fewer local residents would be affected if something went wrong.

By 1943, construction had begun on the building of Naval Ammunition Depot Earle, named after Rear Admiral Ralph Earle, the chief of the Bureau of Ordnance during World War I. The entire facility continued to be developed even after World War II. The depot's name was changed to Naval Weapons Station Earle in 1974.

END OF THE WAR

Only the dead have seen the end of war.
—*Philosopher George Santayana*

In Berlin, Joseph Stalin's Russian forces were successfully moving through the German capital. Adolf Hitler knew the end was near as they approached the bunker where he was hiding. Hitler committed suicide on April 30, 1945. Germany surrendered unconditionally in May 1945. The Japanese weren't ready to give up until August, when atomic bombs were dropped on two of their major cities. The world war was over.

21

THE DEFENDERS

THE COLD WAR

Here's my strategy on the Cold War: We win, they lose.
—President Ronald Reagan

Early in the Cold War, the Soviet Union developed long-range bombers that could reach the United States soon after the Russians exploded their first atomic bomb in 1949. Among the most-threatened targets were harbors, naval bases and industrial centers. For the third time in half a century, New York once again found itself in the crosshairs of an attack plan.

The mission of the Nike surface-to-air missile program was to act as a final line of air defense for selected areas, like New York City. The Nike system would have been used if the U.S. Air Force's interceptor aircraft failed. With some air-to-ground capability with the later Nike Hercules, which was nuclear-capable, these would be the last fixed-fortification weapons employed in the United States.

Joseph Stalin, who was the leader of the Soviet Union until 1953, was upset about his county's lack of intelligence regarding the development of the atomic bomb by the United States. He found out about it when everyone else learned about its devastating power: when it was dropped on Japan to end the war. Immediately, he demanded that his scientists develop a nuclear weapon for his own country. And after the device was tested, the nuclear arms race began in earnest between the two so-called superpowers of the world.

Generally, many historians say the Cold War began in 1947, and its cause and its history are intertwined in a series of complex political, militaristic and economic events. Even the Space Race became part of the global competition between Russia and America.

The Soviet Union consolidated its control over individual countries, collectively the Eastern Bloc. The United States implemented a strategy to challenge Soviet power by trying to contain it. As such, we provided military and financial aid to countries in Western Europe. We also created the NATO alliance, which did not include Russia. Back and forth, both sides went for at least a decade with one world crisis after another.

The Cuban Missile Crisis occurred in 1962, and it would be the closest we would ever come to engaging Russia in a nuclear war. Many folks living in Florida at the time felt like they were living in the bull's-eye of an enemy target.

Meanwhile, during the Cold War, military and government shelters were being built all over the country. Even AT&T, my employer of twenty-five years, was building underground hardened sites to protect the nation's communications system on behalf of the government.

The Cold War era brought a change from antiaircraft guns to Nike missiles on Sandy Hook, New Jersey, that could intercept jet warplanes. Nike sites were built during the 1950s in rings around major urban and industrial areas and critical bases of the Strategic Air Command. They were controlled by the U.S. Army's Air Defense Command, or ARADCOM. Frequently, they were located within heavily populated areas.

Unfortunately, in 1958, a Nike base in Leonardo, New Jersey, with eight fully armed Ajax missiles, blew up in an explosion, killing ten people. The explosion scattered armed warheads across a wide area of the countryside. A twelve-foot section of one missile landed in someone's backyard almost a mile away. The disaster was described by a military spokesperson as an accident that should not have happened, but it did. According to a newspaper report: "Mangled bodies and fragments lay strewn about where a moment before men had stood."

The disintegration of the victims made it challenging to establish identities. In the end, six soldiers and four civilians were dead. Three others were injured, one seriously. Two servicemen in a twenty-foot-deep pit under a missile's launching pad miraculously survived but were treated for shock and hysteria.

Army photograph of damage from Nike Missile Explosion.

Meanwhile, across from Highlands, New Jersey, and on the eastern side of the Shrewsbury River on Sandy Hook were nuclear-tipped warheads on many Nike Hercules missiles located in underground magazines, which could quickly surface to be launched toward any incoming enemy target. People living in Highlands and everywhere else, for that matter, knew almost nothing about these missiles.

Bill Jackson worked here during the Cold War and today volunteers to take groups on tours of the abandoned facility. At one time, this was one of the most highly classified secret locations in the United States. It was a Nike missile base, which was the last role Fort Hancock would play in guarding New York and the surrounding area.

AT&T Bell Laboratories, which was located near Raritan Bay, had helped develop the Nike missile, which was a surface-to-air projectile guided by radar and a tracking computer.

The Nike program started in 1945 soon after the Soviet Union tested its first nuclear bomb. It had also successfully developed a long-range bomber capable of flying more than ten thousand miles. The Nike Ajax missile was about thirty-two feet long and a foot in diameter. It weighed nearly a ton and was designed to bring down enemy aircraft flying up to fifteen miles away at altitudes of up to sixty thousand feet. Typically, these missiles carried three conventional warheads of explosives and shrapnel but were soon replaced by Hercules missiles capable of carrying nuclear warheads.

So these Nike missiles could shoot down what we called the Soviet Bear Bomber. My friend Bill Jackson recalled for me when he and his compatriots at the Nike base went on high alert after their radar indicated a Soviet Bear Bomber was heading toward our air space.

Suddenly, he was preparing the Nike missiles for launch. This was not part of a training drill. This was real, and he was sweating bullets. Before long, the high-alert status was eliminated, and the missiles were deactivated. Whew! That was a close one. What many of us don't realize is this kind of stuff had happened many times in the past, but we just never knew it. It could be happening today.

By the 1970s, these Nike missiles were obsolete, so more than 250 Nike bases throughout the United States were closed. Before long, the United States and Russia were beginning to embrace the concept of peace and stepping away from annihilating each other and the planet in mutually assured destruction and looking for ways to create a safer world. In the early 1970s, the first nuclear arms limitation treaties between us were signed.

Finally, in 1982, one million protesters gathered in New York City to protest the nuclear arms race. Almost ten years later, we saw the dissolution of the USSR and the collapse of communist regimes in other countries. The United States found the last chair in which to sit during the global game of musical chairs. As a result, we soon became the world's only superpower.

22

THE POLLUTERS

POLLUTING RARITAN BAY

In our every deliberation, we must consider the impact of our decisions on the next seven generations.

—Iroquois maxim

In time, we may conclude that the Russians or the Chinese can't destroy us. We may simply destroy ourselves by polluting our environment. And now with climate change, the stakes are even higher unless you don't believe it.

The now-dead oysters may have witnessed what we're capable of doing but had no voices to warn us. It seems as though our ancestors were not smart enough to realize how they were polluting the world. Are we smart enough now? We'll soon see.

There was a time, not so long ago, when we actually thought it was perfectly okay to pour chemicals into our rivers and streams. Hey, it all ends up in the ocean, and we don't have to worry about it.

RARITAN ARSENAL

During World War I, the Raritan Arsenal building along the Raritan River was a polluter. The arsenal continued to be utilized and expanded for storing ammunition during World War II. By the 1950s, many activities at the arsenal were discontinued. Unfortunately, some of the facility's waste, such as ordnance and chemicals that had been buried below ground or burned in a pit, now created many contaminated areas. The arsenal was declared surplus and closed in 1964. At the time, it consisted of more than 3,000 acres with some 440 buildings and 62 miles of roads and railways.

Today, the U.S. Corps of Engineers has started cleaning up the polluted areas. Presently, several entities are located on the site: Thomas A. Edison County Park, Middlesex County College, Raritan Center and the Environmental Protection Agency offices. On the northern section of the site, a number of the original arsenal buildings have been repurposed for other uses. The southern part is mostly wetlands and is closed. As a result, development is limited, and the cleanup process still continues.

RARITAN BAY SLAG

While Raritan Bay was flourishing with marshes, oysters and a variety of resort towns, it was soon feeling the effects of an industrial transformation that began in the early 1920s.

One of the first companies responsible for polluting our environment was the National Lead Company, which became the most extensive lead company in the United States. It was best known for its white-lead paints, which were sold under the Dutch Boy™ label.

One of its many facilities was located in Perth Amboy, a town on the western edge of Raritan Bay, where it operated a lead smelter that generated wastes containing lead and other hazardous substances.

ATLANTIC RESOURCES CORPORATION AND HORSESHOE ROAD

The Horseshoe Road site is a twelve-acre property located in Sayreville, New Jersey, that includes three areas: the Sayreville Pesticide Dump, the former Atlantic Development Corporation facility and the Horseshoe Road Drum Dump. These separate but related sites were among those named by federal officials during a 2014 hearing in Washington, D.C.

An EPA official told Senator Cory Booker and other lawmakers the agency had spent $46.5 million cleaning up the sites and would need another $34 million to finish the job. It's still not thoroughly cleaned up.

CORNELL-DUBILIER ELECTRONICS

Cornell-Dubilier Electronics Inc. operated in South Plainfield, New Jersey, from 1936 to 1962. The company dumped polychlorinated biphenyl (PCB)–contaminated materials, such as capacitors, and so today, the area is listed as a Superfund site. Unfortunately, some of the contamination spread after the company closed down in 1962. PCBs—banned by the EPA in 1979—can cause cancer and affect the nervous, immune, reproductive and endocrine systems. Hundreds of acres of wetlands and streams were contaminated with PCBs and other toxins. Many of these contaminants found their way into Raritan Bay.

AMERICAN CYANAMID

In 1915, American Cyanamid began operations in Bridgewater Township. This company was manufacturing chemicals and then disposing contaminated sludge on its property. The EPA designated the area adjacent to the Raritan River and above the Brunswick Aquifer as a Superfund site. The soil and groundwater have been contaminated with toxic materials, harmful metals and other dangerous chemicals. The company closed the site in 1999.

JOHNS MANVILLE COMPANY

Federal Creosote Site (Johns Manville Company) was located in Manville where a wood treatment facility was in operation from 1910 to the mid-1950s. The plant was treating railroad ties with coal tar (creosote) and then discharging residual chemicals into two local canals. The chemicals were allowed to enter a few bodies of water near the property. In the mid-1960s, the property was redeveloped on top of the contaminated soil. In 1988, the entire property was designated as a Superfund site by the EPA.

MIDDLESEX SAMPLING PLANT

The Middlesex Sampling Plant was located in Middlesex on a ten-acre site with the Manhattan Engineer District and Atomic Energy Commission responsible for its operation from 1943 to 1967. Both radiological and chemical contamination were found on the site during the 1980s. Also found were particulates of uranium and radium, as well as arsenic, chromium, and lead along with several volatile compounds. The site was finally listed as Superfund site in 1999, and the Department of Energy will be responsible for the long-term surveillance, operation and maintenance of the site once the U.S. Army Corps of Engineers has completed remediation.

HERCULES CHEMICAL

Hercules Chemical (Aqualon Parlin Plant) was located in Parlin on a 670-acre chemical facility owned by Dupont and initially built by Union Powder Company in the late 1800s. Hercules purchased the plant in 1915.

In 2006, results from samples of drinking water taken by Sayreville Borough were found to have trace levels of perfluorooctanoic acid (sounds dangerous), which the facility manufactured. Even low levels of exposure to this type of acid are a matter of concern because it doesn't break down and accumulates in the body. Residents and plant employees who are exposed to extremely low levels over time can end up with levels in their blood many times higher.

EDGEBORO LANDFILL

Edgeboro Landfill was located in East Brunswick and privately owned until its closure and capping in the late 1980s. Then, in the 1990s, the area on top and near the site became the state's most massive active waste dump. At one time, it received 700,000 tons of garbage a year. The current facility is run by the Middlesex County Utilities Authority and is projected to remain open until 2024. Keep an eye on it.

KIN-BUCK LANDFILL

Kin-Buck Landfill is located in Edison, New Jersey, where seventy million gallons of liquid toxic waste and one million tons of municipal, industrial and hazardous waste were dumped into the local waterways from the 1940s to 1976. This landfill is one of the largest Superfund sites in New Jersey and is heavily contained with PCBs. This contamination leaked into Edmonds Creek, a tributary of the Raritan River, which flows into Raritan Bay.

ACCIDENTS

[Sinking] *will never happen to me.*

—captain of the Titanic

In addition to companies contributing to the pollution of our waterways, some companies also had their share of accidents. For example, four barges with railroad cars loaded with 420 tons of military explosives accidentally detonated while at the Raritan River Port of South Amboy, New Jersey, in 1950.

The four barges, the railroad cars, the piers and the equipment nearby on the waterfront were utterly destroyed. Also, more than seventeen barges in the area caught on fire or sank. A witness reported that the sky was "cluttered with debris" that looked like cement blocks and railroad ties.

Many of the dockworkers were killed. In all, 31 people died, while more than 350 people were injured by the explosions. The blast destroyed many businesses and homes. It blew out windows and knocked out electrical power. In total, there was more than $10 million in damage to properties.

Immediately, local officials declared a state of emergency in South Amboy. The state police, the Red Cross, military personnel and many volunteers from neighboring towns came to help. A comprehensive investigation of the accident was immediately planned.

Apparently, the Kilgore Manufacturing Company had manufactured 9,000 containers of landmines that were headed to Pakistan. Another company, the Hercules Powder Company, was sending a shipment of 1,800 cases of gelatin dynamite to Afghanistan. Combined, both of these companies were carrying 300,000 pounds of explosive products.

Aftermath of explosion of barges in South Amboy.

At the time, South Amboy was the only terminal in the area that allowed explosives in large quantities to be handled at its pier.

Three years after the incident, some sixty-two live landmines were found scattered throughout the waterfront area. This disaster led to a congressional investigation in which both companies were indicted and charged with violations.

But enough about what we've done to our planet. Let's talk about Mother Nature.

23

THE WEATHER

MOTHER NATURE

We live, we die, and like the grass and trees, renew ourselves from the soft earth of the grave. Stones crumble and decay, faiths grow old and they are forgotten, but new beliefs are born. The faith of the villages is dust now… but it will grow again…like the trees.

—Chief Joseph, Nez Perce

We know the great influence humans have had in modifying or even removing the natural landforms and waterways. Many of the marshes and swamps have been filled in to be more suitable for building structures. Many of the trees have been felled to clear the land for even more building of structures and highways.

Most trees in our area live to be 20 to 50 years old. In other parts of the country, like the giant redwoods in California, they may live up to 2,000 years. In eastern North American, the most long-lived species is the bald cypress (*Taxodium distichum)*, which grows fifty to seventy feet tall. There's one in North Carolina that's known to have lived at least 1,622 years.

Unfortunately, one of New Jersey's oldest trees succumbed to Mother Nature's will when it was uprooted and fell for no apparent reason next to a graveyard. Many of Salem's earliest residents were buried in the graveyard under the tree's broad branches.

Could this be the tree in Salem where the treaty was made?

It was called the Salem Oak Tree, estimated to be between five and six hundred years old. It was listed as the tallest white oak tree in New Jersey. Many believe the tree was located where Quaker John Fenwick, the man who brought the first English settlement to West Jersey in 1675, brokered a peace treaty with the Lenape Indians.

FINAL THOUGHTS

MY OWN THEORY OF RELATIVITY

Two things are infinite: the universe and human stupidity; and I'm not sure about the universe.

—Albert Einstein

Einstein was not only smart, he was funny as well. He lived in Princeton, New Jersey, from 1935 until his death in 1955.

He loved sailing, even though he wasn't very good at it. His friends on Long Island frequently had to help him when he capsized his boat *Tinef* (Yiddish for "Worthless"). And even though Einstein never learned to swim, he kept sailing as a hobby throughout his life. Perhaps he enjoyed boating on Raritan Bay.

Einstein published his theory of general relativity in 1915. By 1922, scientists used his theory to show the universe must be either expanding or contracting. Within a decade, many of these scientists believed that Einstein's theory of an expanding universe could be traced back to a single point in time.

In 1964, two American radio astronomers were experimenting on the highest point in Monmouth County in New Jersey. It was Crawford Hill, which is some 391 feet tall. There, they discovered that the very first beams of light were created from a tremendous cosmic explosion, which essentially created the universe.

Left: Radio Telescope on Crawford Hill. *Right*: Albert Einstein.

Thanks to them, I started my stories for you at a single point in time when the universe began about thirteen billion years ago. And here's where I will end it. I don't really have any stories to tell before the Big Bang, and I don't really have any stories at this time going forward. Except to say…

OUR PRECIOUS MEMORIES

As we begin getting older, I think our interest in history begins to develop more fully because we start to look at our own past as historical. And as our consciousness of mortality threatens our security about living forever, and we realize we have fewer years ahead of us than behind us, our own unique history sometimes becomes a comfortable emotional pillow on which to rest our heads if our memories are pleasant enough.

And while we do realize the inherent flaws in our memories, which sometimes only capture the best of times from our past, we deliberately allow this self-filtering of adverse events to assure ourselves a good night's sleep on that emotional pillow.

The historical landscape of our collective social consciousness is as varied as we tend to be: colors, shapes, sizes, languages, points of view and, of course, the list goes on. The dates, places, names, facts and figures, however, are primarily contained in layers of firm historical sediment. They rarely change over time and are generally not open to interpretation. They have no context and no perspective from which to draw a picture of what happened and why.

That's why the photographs and images from our past become essential pieces of a puzzle we try to solve by creating stories in our minds, which help to explain what we see or read. It's a way for us to make sense of what we are taught about history.

But history is vast like the universe. Where does one begin to start the process of gaining access to the knowledge historians have gathered to enlighten us? Yes, we can read a lot of books, watch a lot of documentary films, do our own research on the internet, attend lectures or join historical groups.

Some people, however, turn to themselves as the closest resource. They look through an old shoebox of undocumented photographs where perhaps they find a name or place etched on the back of a square photo with scalloped edges. Today, of course, most of these collections have been replaced with images captured on the phone.

My grandparents had such a box full of old photographs that captured my imagination. I would ask who was who and what was what. The photographs were spread across the floor in front of me, where I sat in wonder as my curiosity developed into a passion for exploring my own past. Who were these people? How did I relate to them? What were they thinking? Was I like any of them? And then I would carefully stare into the photograph as the background became more evident, and I could imagine where they were standing.

A retouched selfie by Robert Cornelius, 1839. *Courtesy of Jill Kramer.*

Unfortunately, so many of our family collections of photographs have been lost or tossed from existence. And sadly, today's collections of images in modern cellular phones may share a similar fate for altogether different reasons. And I'm not even sure of how many people today even care about keeping photographs in their phones or protecting any old photographs in shoeboxes that were lucky enough to survive the ravages of time.

I must confess: I haven't always followed my own desire to document my personal history. I have boxes, albums and computer file folders of personal photographs, but have done little to identify the pictures. Sadly, I don't believe my children really care that much about my past—or even theirs. Perhaps as they become older, their interest may grow, but it may be too late to have thought ahead enough to start their own collection of photographs in a proverbial shoebox.

In 1839, Louis Daguerre invented the camera and became known as the father of modern photography. The oldest known photographic self-portrait (selfie) is that of Robert Cornelius, who snapped his own portrait in the same year as the camera was invented. He looks like quite the proverbial swashbuckler. Lucky for him, he didn't have to sit for an extended period to be painted.

While our humble beginnings are far less impressive than what lies as ruins in ancient Greece or the still-standing architectural masterpieces of Europe, we have still enough standing and lying about to remind us of our own unique history. And we have lots more to explore, which may help us understand who we were and what we have become.

WHO AM I?

As the founder and executive producer of a weekly television series called *Raritan Bayshore Living*, which appears on Comcast and several social media on the internet, I enjoy bringing to life some of the history that occurred all around—no matter where we live.

I genuinely love sharing the local beauty and colorful history of this area to help people understand and appreciate the relics and spirits of the past that surround them. And I have invested a considerable amount of time, energy and financial resources in doing so without seeking any financial return for my efforts.

Since retiring as a marketing executive with AT&T, I have made this area my home. I started my campaign to position our area as a great place to live, work and play out of my considerable love for the region of New Jersey and New York where I live. That's why my mission since Hurricane Sandy struck this area has been to show people their ancestral roots and relics.

And while some people would like to keep out the tourists who invade us every summer, I want to welcome them with open arms for a variety of reasons.

Today, more than one million people every year see my television program of travelogues and historical documentaries. My weekly program—available to Comcast subscribers in Toms River, Ocean, Monmouth and Union Counties—has featured episodes on the Revolutionary War, tours of local

The author with his camera.

towns and villages, interviews with newsmakers and celebrities, walking tours and things many folks never knew about.

And I am always conscientious of all our ancestral spirits who were so different than us. I cannot imagine what fortitude they embraced to make our country hospitable. They weren't perfect, but I'm not sure we can describe ourselves as being perfect. We, like them, have a great deal to learn about how to be better at living and connecting with those who live in our community.

There are so many dark sides to our history throughout the Raritan Bay area: wars, slavery, pollution, greed, politics and our treatment of the Africans and Native Americans.

I cannot imagine how a human being, no matter what color, could be treated as property. It was accepted by so many as a normal part of life, however. It's a deplorable part of our history.

I'm also regretful and sad about the way we collectively treated the Native Americans when we invaded their space and stripped them of their dignity.

I don't mean to preach but simply invoke the historical memory of how difficult life must have been for most people coming to America during the very early days.

I must confess, as a parent, I preach to my daughter once in a while. I like to consider it sharing my feelings, but she may view it differently. Regardless, I shared with her (or preached) my feelings about the "meaning of life." I could see her fasten an emotional seatbelt as I inhaled deeply to begin my sermon.

"Life," I began "is full of adventures." God, I hope she doesn't bolt, I thought. I continued cautiously.

"And sometimes you'll have good experiences, and sometimes you'll experience the bad." Duh, I could see her thinking, so I went for the punch line, which required me to set aside religious faith.

"In the end, we are left with only the memories of what we actually experienced and dreamed along the way." So far, so good, I thought.

"And in that final moment of our lives, a great tsunami of memories will wash over us like a flood of everything we were and everything we experienced and felt. It all comes rushing into our final moments of consciousness and then kisses us goodbye for eternity."

My daughter looked at me and said, "Okay, Dad. Thanks."

I've reminded her many times as she continues on her journey. I think she gets it.

So, my friends, if that's what happens during our last breath, then we'd better make every moment count while we're living. We should avoid the negative and embrace the positive. When we begin our journey to wherever we go, we want to make sure the net gain of our lives is in the plus column.

Shawnee chief
Tecumseh
(1768–1813).

As you may have noticed, I used a few translated quotes from some of the American Indians because they were pretty good quotes, but I also didn't want anyone to forget them while writing these stories.

My favorite quote is from Tecumseh (1768–1813), a Shawnee chief and warrior who fought the United States after forming an alliance with Great Britain in the War of 1812. Tecumseh was killed in battle in 1813.

Tecumseh was well known as a strong and well-spoken man who always promoted the unity of all tribes. He was also ambitious, willing to take risks and to make significant sacrifices to stop Americans from seizing the land of Native Americans. Who could blame him?

Here's what he said:

> *Live your life that the fear of death can never enter your heart.*
> *Trouble no one about his religion.*
> *Respect others in their views and demand that they respect yours.*
> *Love your life, perfect your life, beautify all things in your life.*
> *Seek to make your life long and of service to your people.*
> *Prepare a noble death song for the day when you go over the great divide.*
> *Always give a word or sign of salute when meeting or passing a friend, or even a stranger, if in a lonely place.*
> *Show respect to all people, but grovel to none.*
> *When you rise in the morning, give thanks for the light, for your life, for your strength.*
> *Give thanks for your food and for the joy of living.*
> *If you see no reason to give thanks, the fault lies in yourself.*
> *Touch not the poisonous firewater that makes wise ones turn to fools and robs their spirit of its vision.*
> *When your time comes to die, be not like those whose hearts are filled with fear of death, so that when their time comes they weep and pray for a little more time to live their lives over again in a different way.*
> *Sing your death song, and die like a hero going home.*

Amen, say I.

ONE MORE THING

Thank you for reading everything printed before the words you're reading now. And before you turn the final page, please know how much I enjoyed

Raritan Bay and the many waterways that enter it.

spending time with you in *The Casalecki*. It may sound like I'm using the creative license many writers utilize to make their work more interesting. Perhaps I am, but not entirely. As I wrote and rewrote this book, I did think of you and me in my boat. And I characterized you as someone who shares my sense of how vital and exciting our histories can be. You have yours, and I have mine. And while we may view things differently, I had the sense we were mostly together in our mutual appreciation of what we experienced and felt during the preceding stories.

I always enjoy creating historical documentaries that are shared during my weekly program on cable television as well as posted in a variety of social media. At the end of my show, I always thank everyone for watching. Then I remind them of what I always say at the end of every episode: "If you see me somewhere when you're out and about, don't hesitate to tap me on the shoulder and introduce yourself because nothing is more important than meeting you."

Dear reader, I invite you to do the same. Sincerely, John

ACKNOWLEDGEMENTS

Colonel Shawn Welch
Thomas Minton
William Schultz
Wanda Radowski
Diane Quinn
Gary Saretsky
Robert A. Mayers
Rick Geffken
Muriel Smith
Randall Gabriellan
Les Horner
Tom Gallo
The Dorn Family
Walt Guenther
Cory Newman
Tom Hoffman
Susan Gardiner
Jennifer Cox
Al Savolaine
Monmouth County Historical Archives
Army Ground Forces Association
New York/New Jersey Baykeeper
National Park Service

BIBLIOGRAPHY

Ellis, Franklin. *History of Monmouth County*. Philadelphia: R.T. Peck, 1885.

Gabrielan, Randall. *Monmouth County Historic Landmarks*. Charleston, SC: The History Press, 2011.

———. *Monmouth County, New Jersey*. Postcard History Series. Charleston, SC: Arcadia Publishing, 1998.

Gallo, Tom. *Henry Hudson Trail*. Charleston, SC: Arcadia Publishing, 1999.

Gallo, Tom, and William B. Longo. *Railroads of Monmouth County*. Charleston, SC: Arcadia Publishing, 2007.

Geffken, Rick, and George Severini. *Lost Amusement Parks of the Jersey Shore*. Charleston, SC: The History Press, 2017.

Geffken, Rick, and Muriel J. Smith. *Hidden History of Monmouth County*. Charleston, SC: The History Press, 2019.

Hoffman, Thomas. *Fort Hancock*. Charleston, SC: Arcadia Publishing, 2007.

Kobbe, Gustav. *The Central Railroad of New Jersey*. N.p.: Dalton House, 2018.

Mayers, Robert A. *Revolutionary New Jersey*. Staunton, VA: American History Press, 2018.

———. *Searching for Yankee Doodle*. Staunton, VA: American History Press, 2016.

———. *The War Man*. Yardley, PA: Westholme Publishing, 2009.

Moss, George H., Jr. *Navoo to the Hook*. Locust, NJ: Jervey Close Press, 1964.

Nagiewicz, Captain Stephen D. *Hidden History of Maritime New Jersey*. Charleston, SC: The History Press, 2016.

Salter, Edwin. *History of Monmouth and Ocean Counties*. Bayonne, NJ: E. Gardner & Son, 1890.

Savolaine, John Allan. *Stanley Fisher: Shark Attack Hero*. N.p.: Riverside Prints, 2016.

Sayreville Historical Society. *Sayreville*. Charleston, SC: Arcadia Publishing, 2001.

Slesinski, Jason J. *Along the Raritan River*. Charleston, SC: Arcadia Publishing, 2014.

Tottenville Historical Society. *Tottenville*. Charleston, SC: Arcadia Publishing, 2011.

ABOUT THE AUTHOR

John is a former marketing executive at AT&T who has devoted his retired life to sharing public and local history through a variety of media. For example, he hosts a weekly television program seen on social media and cable television in a number of counties along the Jersey Shore called *Raritan Bayshore Living*. His programs may be also viewed at www. RaritanBayshoreLiving.com. Recently, he was honored to be one of the top fifty historians in Monmouth County (New Jersey) during the last fifty years.